T0392270

SpringerBriefs in Computer Science

SpringerBriefs present concise summaries of cutting-edge research and practical applications across a wide spectrum of fields. Featuring compact volumes of 50 to 125 pages, the series covers a range of content from professional to academic.

Typical topics might include:

- A timely report of state-of-the art analytical techniques
- A bridge between new research results, as published in journal articles, and a contextual literature review
- A snapshot of a hot or emerging topic
- An in-depth case study or clinical example
- A presentation of core concepts that students must understand in order to make independent contributions

Briefs allow authors to present their ideas and readers to absorb them with minimal time investment. Briefs will be published as part of Springer's eBook collection, with millions of users worldwide. In addition, Briefs will be available for individual print and electronic purchase. Briefs are characterized by fast, global electronic dissemination, standard publishing contracts, easy-to-use manuscript preparation and formatting guidelines, and expedited production schedules. We aim for publication 8–12 weeks after acceptance. Both solicited and unsolicited manuscripts are considered for publication in this series.

**Indexing: This series is indexed in Scopus, Ei-Compendex, and zbMATH **

Itsuo Takanami

Self-restructuring in Fault Tolerant Architecture

Processor Arrays with Spares

 Springer

Itsuo Takanami
Yamaguchi University
Yamaguchi, Japan

ISSN 2191-5768   ISSN 2191-5776 (electronic)
SpringerBriefs in Computer Science
ISBN 978-981-96-1538-4   ISBN 978-981-96-1539-1 (eBook)
https://doi.org/10.1007/978-981-96-1539-1

© The Author(s), under exclusive license to Springer Nature Singapore Pte Ltd. 2025

This work is subject to copyright. All rights are solely and exclusively licensed by the Publisher, whether the whole or part of the material is concerned, specifically the rights of translation, reprinting, reuse of illustrations, recitation, broadcasting, reproduction on microfilms or in any other physical way, and transmission or information storage and retrieval, electronic adaptation, computer software, or by similar or dissimilar methodology now known or hereafter developed.
The use of general descriptive names, registered names, trademarks, service marks, etc. in this publication does not imply, even in the absence of a specific statement, that such names are exempt from the relevant protective laws and regulations and therefore free for general use.
The publisher, the authors and the editors are safe to assume that the advice and information in this book are believed to be true and accurate at the date of publication. Neither the publisher nor the authors or the editors give a warranty, expressed or implied, with respect to the material contained herein or for any errors or omissions that may have been made. The publisher remains neutral with regard to jurisdictional claims in published maps and institutional affiliations.

This Springer imprint is published by the registered company Springer Nature Singapore Pte Ltd.
The registered company address is: 152 Beach Road, #21-01/04 Gateway East, Singapore 189721, Singapore

If disposing of this product, please recycle the paper.

Preface

In recent years, there has been a rapidly growing interest in processing many kinds of vast amount of information in real-time and near-real-time. The demand for strengthening computation power will never stop, and it is increasing day by day. For these needs, how to realize high-speed and massively parallel computers has been the subject of extensive research. A mesh-connected processor array (PA) is a kind of form of massively parallel computers. Mesh-connected PAs consisting of hundreds of processing elements (PEs) offer a regular and modular structure, a small wiring length between PEs, and a high scalability, thus very suitable for most signal and image processing algorithms.

As VLSI technology has developed, the realization of parallel computing systems using multi-chip module (MCM), e.g., [1], wafer scale integration (WSI), e.g., [2] or network-on-chip (NoC), e.g., [3] has been considered so as to enhance the computation and communication performance, decrease energy consumption and sizes, and so on. In such a realization, entire or significant parts of PEs and interconnections among them are implemented on a single chip or wafer. Therefore, the yield and/or reliability of the system may become drastically low if no strategy is employed for coping with defects and faults. In such systems, if a single PE fails to perform its assigned task correctly due to some defects/faults, the entire computation will result in failure or computing speed will be down. Hence, it is important to make high reliable systems which are called "fault-tolerant computer systems". In order to restore the correct computation capabilities of the systems with faults, they must be restructured appropriately using spare PEs so that the faulty PEs are eliminated from the computation paths by replacing faulty PEs with healthy spare PEs and the remaining healthy PEs maintain correct logical connectivity among them.

Various strategies to restructure a faulty physical system into a fault-free target logical system are described in the literature, e.g., [1, 3, 4, 6, 7, 8, 9, 10, 11, 12, 14, 15]. Some of these techniques employ very powerful restructuring systems that can repair a faulty PA with almost certainty, even in the presence of clusters of multiple faults. However, the key limitation of these techniques is that they are executed in software programs to run on an external host computer and they cannot be designed and implemented efficiently within a system. If a faulty system can be self-restructured by a built-in circuit or network, the system downtime is significantly reduced. Furthermore, the system will become more reliable when it is used in such an environment that the fault information cannot be monitored externally and manual maintenance operations are difficult.

This book concerns self-restructuring in fault-tolerant computer systems consisting of many processor elements (PEs), mainly mesh-connected processor arrays with spares, where "self-restructuring" implies that the restructuring is done without an external host computer, using built-in circuits. The architectures are described in terms of the number of spares as well as spare arrangements, replacement algorithms, and the network structures with built-in circuits. The degrees of fault-tolerance are evaluated in terms of survival rates and reliabilities.

Yamaguchi, Japan   Itsuo Takanami

References

1. Schaper, L.W.: Design of multichip modules, Proceedings of the IEEE, vol. 80, Issue 12, pp. 1955–1964, (1992)
2. Okamoto, K.: Importance of wafer bonding for the future hype-miniaturized cmos devices. ECS Transactions, vol. 16, No. 8, pp. 15–29, (2008)
3. Dally, W.J., Towles, B.: Route Packets, Not Wires: On-chip Interconnection Networks Proceedings of the 38th Design Automation Conference, pp. 684–689, 2001, March, (2001)
4. Mangir, E., Avizienis, A.: Fault-Tolerant Design for VLSI: Effect of Interconnection Requirements on Yield Improvement of VLSI Designs IEEE Trans. on Computer, vol. c-31, No. 7, pp. 609–615, July, (1982)
5. Leighton, T., Leiserson, E.: Wafer-scale integration of systolic arrays. IEEE Trans. Comput., vol. C-34, No. 5, pp. 448–461, May, (1985)
6. M. Sami R. Negrini and R. Stefanelli. Fault tolerance techniues for array structures used in supercomputing. IEEE Computer, Vol. 19, No. 2, pp. 78–87, February, (1986)
7. Sami, M., Stefanelli, R.: Reconfigurable Architectures for VLSI Processing Arrays, Proc. IEEE, pp. 712–722, May, (1986)
8. Shigei, N., Miyajima, H., Murashima, S.: On Efficient spare arrangement and an algorithm with relocating spares for reconfiguring processor arrays, IEICE Tran. Fundamentals, vol. E80-A, no. 6, pp. 988–995, June, (1997)
9. Kung, S.Y., Jean, S.N., Chang, C.W.: Fault-Tolerant Array Processors Using Single-Track Switches. IEEE Trans.Comput., vol. 38, No. 4, pp. 501–514, January, (1989)
10. Negrini, R., Sami M.G., Stefanelli, R.: Fault-tolerance through reconfiguration of VLSI and WSI arrays, MIT Press series in computer systems, MIT Press, (1989)
11. Roychowdhury, V.P., Bruck, J., KailathT.: Efficient Algorithms for Reconstruction in VLSI/ WSI Array, IEEE Trans.Comput., vol. 39, No. 4, pp. 480–489, April, (1989)
12. Lam, C.W.H., Li, H.F., Jakakumar, R.: A study of two approaches for reconfiguring fault-tolerant systolic arrays. IEEE Trans. Comput., vol. 38, No. 6, pp. 833–844, June, (1989)
13. Kim, J.H., Reddy, S.M.: On the design of fault-tolerant two-dimensional systolic arrays for yield enhancement. IEEE Trans. Comput., vol. 38, No. 4, pp. 515–525, April, (1989)
14. Koren, I., Singh, A.D.: Fault Tolerance in VLSI Circuits, IEEE Computer, pp. 73–83, July, (1990)
15. Hideo Ito, Array Structure Using Basic Wiring Channels for WSI Hypercube, IEICE Trans. on INF & SYST. in Japan, vol. E75-D, No. 6, pp. 884–893, November, (1992)

Contents

Chapter 1
Introduction

Abstract The arrangements of processor elements (PEs) in the typical arrays such as line array, two-dimensional array, three-dimensional array and tree array are shown. If array systems have no spares and a single PE fails to perform its assigned task correctly due to some defects/faults, the computation will result in failure or computing speed will be down. To confirm this situation, the reliabilities of two-dimensional arrays with sizes of $N \times N (N = 4, 8, 16)$ are shown.

Keywords Fault tolerance · One-dimensional array · Two-dimensional array · Three-dimensional array · Spares · Reliability

Figure 1.1 shows arrangements of processor elements (PEs) in the typical arrays. They are (a) line array, (b) 2D array, (c) 3D array, (d) tree array, and so on.

  If array systems have no spares and a single PE fails to perform its assigned task correctly due to some defects/faults, the computation will result in failure or computing speed will be down. To confirm this situation, Fig. 1.2 shows the reliabilities for 2D arrays with sizes of $N \times N$ ($N = 4, 8, 16$). where the reliability r is given by p^n where p is the reliability of a PE and n is the number of PEs.

  Figure 1.3 shows an array in which each PE consists of three processor elements which have the same function, i.e., two additional PEs per each PE Then, the computation of PE is performed by the majority decision of three processor elements. So, PE works correctly if the number of healthy processor elements is more than or equal to two. Then, the system reliability r is given by $r = (p^3 + 3 \cdot p^2 \cdot (1 - p))^n$ where n is the number of PEs. Figure 1.4 shows the reliabilities for arrays with size of $N \times N$ ($N = 4, 8, 16$). Note that in this system, the number of additional processor elements is $2N^2$.

  By the way, if spares are arranged in an array, their arrangement and the way of replacing faulty PEs with them should be considered. In general, as the number of spares increases, the array reliabilities increase. However, the increase in the number of spares results in those of additional PEs and mechanism for replacing faulty PEs with spares.

  In this book, the arrays with spares shown in Figs. 1.5 and 1.6 are treated with, using the direct replacing and the single track shifting as replacing ways.

© The Author(s), under exclusive license to Springer Nature Singapore Pte Ltd. 2025
I. Takanami, *Self-restructuring in Fault Tolerant Architecture*,
SpringerBriefs in Computer Science, https://doi.org/10.1007/978-981-96-1539-1_1

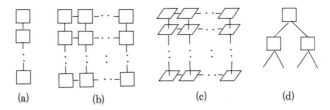

Fig. 1.1 Typical arrays consisting of PEs where **a** line array, **b** 2D mesh array, **c** 3D array and **d** tree array

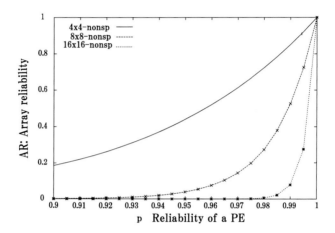

Fig. 1.2 Reliabilities of arrays without spares

Fig. 1.3 An array consisting of PEs each with majority decision

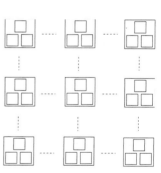

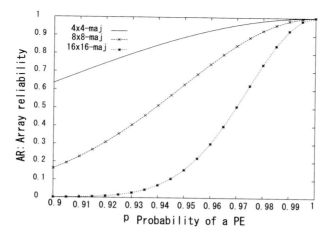

Fig. 1.4 Reliabilities of arrays consisting of PEs each with majority decision

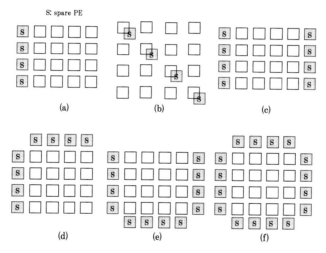

Fig. 1.5 Examples of 2D arrays with spares on the sides

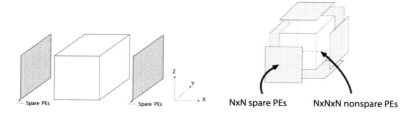

Fig. 1.6 Examples of 3D mesh array with spares on the surfaces

Chapter 2
Two Dimensional Arrays (2D Arrays) with N Spares

Abstract Self-restructuring schemes for $N \times N$ Arrays with N spares on single side and diagonal as spare arrangements are described. Restructuring is done by either direct replacement (DR) or single-track-shift (STS) for the spare arrangements. A restructuring algorithm for the case that faulty PEs are replaced with spares on diagonal by DR is characterized and given as a matching problem in graph theory. For the replacement by STS, a restructuring algorithm satisfying the given repairability condition is shown. A logical circuit to execute each algorithm to be proposed is described. The survival rates and array reliabilities are shown to evaluate the effectiveness of the algorithms.

Keywords Fault-tolerance · Two-dimensional array · Spares on one side · Spares on diagonal · Restructuring · Reconfiguration · Direct replacement · Single-track shift · Built-in circuit

2.1 Spare on Single Side

In a single-side spare scheme (in short, written as SS-scheme), N spares are located on single side of an array with size of $N \times N$. In SS-scheme, a faulty PE is replaced by the spare on the same row. Two replacing methods of direct (DR) and single-track-shift (STS) methods are introduced. Note that the system reliability r is given by $r = [p^{N+1} + (N+1)p^N(1-p)]^N$ for an array with size of $N \times N$ since the system can work well if and only if for each row, the number of faulty PEs is less than two.

© The Author(s), under exclusive license to Springer Nature Singapore Pte Ltd. 2025
I. Takanami, *Self-restructuring in Fault Tolerant Architecture*,
SpringerBriefs in Computer Science, https://doi.org/10.1007/978-981-96-1539-1_2

2.1.1   Restructuring Algorithm by Direct Replacement (RA-SS-DR)

- **Direct replacing (DR) method**

Figure 2.1 shows an interconnection structure of SS-schemes and faulty PEs are replaced directly by healthy spare PEs, switching the sw's around PEs, the behavior of which will be easily seen.

Restructuring algorithm (RA-SS-DR)

Notation 2.1

- PE(i, j) $(1 \leq i \leq N, 1 \leq j \leq N)$ denotes the PE at location (i, j), i.e., the i-row and j-column, in a PA. The notation "PE$[i, j]$" is used when it's physical location must be definitely expressed.
- Spares are assigned on the left side, i.e., $S(k)$ $(1 \leq k \leq N)$ denotes the spare PE at location $(k, 0)$.
- p_{ij} is the fault state of PE(i, j) (spare $S(k)$) where $p_{ij}((s_k))=1$ and $=0$ mean that PE$(i, j)((S(k))$ is faulty and healthy, respectively. (PE(i, j) is also often denoted simply as p_{ij} if no confusion occurs).
- A matrix $P = (p_{ij})$ $(1 \leq i \leq N, 0 \leq j \leq N)$ is called a fault pattern.
- *flg* and *sfg* are flags used in the algorithm.
- "Set the value of A to B" is simply denoted as "Set A to B", if no confusion occurs.

Fig. 2.1 Interconnection structure of SS-scheme by direct replacement

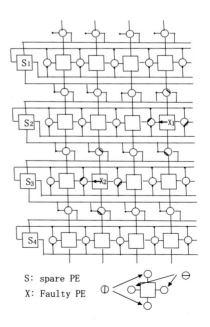

S: spare PE
X: Faulty PE

- If a faulty PE is replaced by a spare PE, it is said to be repaired, otherwise unrepaired
- For a PA with fault pattern P, if all the faults in P can be repaired at the same time, PA as well as P is said to be repairable, otherwise unrepairable.

Do the following steps.

Step 1. Set sfg to 1.
Step 2. Increasing i from 1 to N, do Steps 2-1 to 2-2.

Step 2-1. Set flg to $p_{i0}(=s_i)$.
Step 2-2. Increasing j from 1 to N, do

Step 2-2-1. If (p_{ij}=1 and flg=1), set sfg to 0 and goto Step 3.
Step 2-2-2. If (p_{ij}=1 and flg=0), then set flg to 1.

Step 3. If $sfg = 0$, P is unrepairable, otherwise repairable.
Step 4. End.

2.1.2   Restructuring Algorithm by Single-Track-Shift Replacement

- **Single-track-shift (STS) method**

The replacement of a faulty PE is done as follows. A faulty PE marked with $\times$ denoted in Fig. 2.2 is bypassed in the horizontal directions and replaced by its adjacent healthy PE in the left, which in turn is replaced by the next adjacent healthy PE, and so on. This replacement is repeated until a healthy spare PE is used in the end. This process defines a compensation path (shortly written as c-path), which is a set of straight and continuous PEs from the faulty PE to a healthy spare PE. Note that a c-path is straight and continuous and must not pass other faulty PEs. Figure 2.3 shows an interconnection structure with c-paths and the state of switches where PEs with the mark $\times$ are faulty.

Restructuring algorithm (RA-SS-STS).

- D is a matrix with the same size as that of a fault pattern P.

Fig. 2.2 c-paths in STS for faulty PEs marked with X

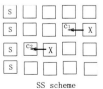

SS scheme

• Do the following steps.

Step 1. Set all the elements of D to 0s and sfg to 1.
Step 2. Increasing i from 1 to N, do Step 2-1 to 2-4.

  Step 2-1. Set flg to $p_{i0}(=s_i)$.
  Step 2-2. Increasing j from 1 to N, do
  Step 2-3 if ($p_{ij}=1$ and $flg=1$), set sfg to 0 and goto Step 3.
  Step 2-4. If ($p_{ij}=1$ and $flg=0$), then

    Step 2-4-1 set flg to 1,
    Step 2-4-2 decreasing k from i to 1, set d_{ik} in D to 1.

Step 3. If $sfg = 0$, P is unrepairable, otherwise repairable.
Step 4 End.   □

    Figure 2.4 illustrates the behavior of CC's executing RA-SS-STS where the faulty
signal of PE is input to the terminal denoted as p in the bottom of CC.

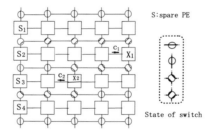

Fig. 2.3 Interconnection structure with c-paths and the state of switches

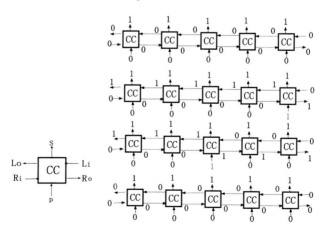

Fig. 2.4 An illustration of behavior of CC's for executing RA-SS-STS

Table 2.1 Truth table of CC for RA-SS-STS ($*$ means *don't care*)

p	R_{in}	L_{in}	R_{out}	L_{out}	$S(= sfg)$
1	0	0	1	1	1
1	0	1	1	1	1
1	1	0	1	$*$	0
1	1	1	1	$*$	0
0	0	0	0	0	1
0	0	1	0	1	1
0	1	0	1	0	1
0	1	1	1	1	1

From Table 2.1, the following equations are obtained.

$$R_{out} = R_{in} + p$$

$$L_{out} = L_{in} + p$$

$$S = \overline{p} + \overline{R}_{in}$$

2.2 Spares on Diagonal with Direct Replacement (DG-DR)

Figure 2.5 shows the diagonal spare arrangement scheme (DG-scheme). Spare PEs are physically or logically located on the diagonal of a mesh-connected array. Note that the spare PEs are not necessarily located physically on the diagonal as to be shown later.

Notation 2.2 • The spare at the address (i, i) on the diagonal is denoted as $S(i)$. Then, the faulty PE[i, j] is replaced by either $S(i)$ or $S(j)$.
• If a faulty PE can be replaced by a healthy spare PE, it is called to be repairable.
□

• Note that a faulty spare PE is considered to be replaced by itself.

Fig. 2.5 Arrangement of PEs in DG-scheme

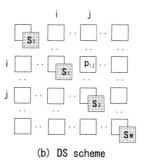

(b) DS scheme

2.2.1 Restructuring Algorithm Using Graph Theory

A faulty PE is directly replaced by a spare. In the following, how to replace all the faulty PEs by healthy spare PEs at the same time will be discussed. It is characterized using a bipartite graph in Graph Theory as follows.

Notation 2.3 • A graph G is defined by a pair of a set V of vertices (points) and a set E of edges (branches) where the edges connect the vertices. Then, G is written as $G=(V, E)$. An edge e which connects vertices u and v is denoted as $e=(u, v)$ in $V \times V$, and the u and v are called to be the vertices of e.
- A subset S of E is called to be **independent** if vertices of e's in E are not shared with each other, i.e., no edges in S are connected to the same vertices.
- A **bipartite graph** $G=(V, E)$ is such a graph that $V = V_1 \cup V_2$, $V_1 \cap V_2 = \phi$ (empty) and the vertices of any e in E is not in V_1 and V_2 at the same time, i.e., if one is in V_1, another is in V_2.
- For $S(\subseteq V_1)$, let denote $\psi(S) = \{v \in V_2 | w \in S, (w, v) \in E\}$.
- The degree of a vertex u is defined as the number of edges incident to u and denoted as $deg(u)$.
- A subset M of E in a bipartite $G=(V_1, V_2, E)$ is called to be a **matching** of G from V_1 to V_2 if it is independent and the vertex set of M in V_1 is equal to V_1.
  □

Compensation graph

For an $N \times N$ PA with faulty PEs, a fault pattern P (= V_f) and V_s are defined such that $V_f = \{p_{ij} \mid \text{PE}[i, j]$ $(1 \le i, j \le N)$ is faulty$\} \cup \{s_k \mid S(k)$ is faulty$\}$ and $V_s = \{s_i, s_j \mid \text{PE}[i, j]$ is faulty$\} \cup \{s_k \mid S(k)$ is faulty$\}$. Then, the compensation (bipartite) graph $G_P = (V, E)$ is defined as $V_1 = V_f$ and $V_2 = V_s$, and $E = \{(p_{ij}, s_i), (p_{ij}, s_j) \mid \text{PE}[i, j]$ $(1 \le i, j \le N)$ is faulty$\} \cup \{(s_k, s_k) \mid S(k)$ $(1 \le k \le N)$ is faulty$\}$ where p_{ij} and s_k are called to be the vertices of $\text{PE}[i, j]$ and $S(k)$, respectively. □

Figure 2.6a shows an example of a fault pattern P where six faulty PEs are marked with X_1 to X_6. (b) is the compensation graph G_P and (c) shows two connected components CC_1 and CC_2 in G_P.

From the compensation graph defined as above, it is clear that the following holds.

Property 2.1 (Repairability condition (RC)) *A fault pattern P is repairable by direct replacement if and only if a matching from V_f to V_s exists. For such a matching M, a faulty PE(i, j) is replaced by spare $S(i)$ if (p_{ij}, s_i) is in M, and by spare $S(j)$ if (p_{ij}, s_j) is in M, and $S(k)$ is replaced by itself if (s_k, s_k) is in M.* □

Further, the following holds.

Property 2.2 *The degree of any faulty vertex is equal to or less than two. Especially, $deg(s) = 1$ for vertex s of faulty spare S and $deg(p) = 2$ for vertex p of faulty nonspare PE.* □

Fig. 2.6 a An example of a fault pattern. **b** Compensation graph. **c** Connected components CC_1 and CC_2

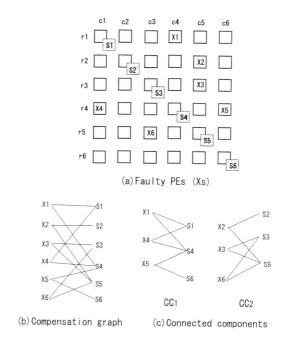

(a) Faulty PEs (Xs)

(b) Compensation graph

(c) Connected components

Using the property, the repairability theorem is given as follows.

Theorem 2.1 (Repairability theorem A) *Let $G = (V, E)$ be a bipartite graph such that $V = V_1 \cup V_2$, $V_1 \cap V_2 = \phi$ and $E \subseteq V_1 \times V_2 (=\{(u, w) \mid u \in V_1, w \in V_2\})$ where the degree of any vertex in V_1 is equal to or less than two. We partition the maximal subgraph of G with the vertex set $V_1 \cup \psi(V_1)$ into connected components and denote the vertex sets in V_1 of the connected components as $C_1, C_2, \ldots, C_m$ (for each C_p, $C_p \subseteq V_1$, $\psi(C_p) \subseteq V_2$, and for $i \neq j$ $(C_i \cup \psi(C_i)) \cap (C_j \cup \psi(C_j)) = \phi$).*

Then, the repairability condition is as follows.

There exists a matching from V_1 to V_2 if and only if $|C_i| \leq |\psi(C_i)|$ for all C_i holds, where $|C|$ means the number of elements of C.

Proof The only-if-part clearly holds. The if-part: we prove by induction on $|C_i|$. It is sufficient to prove that there exists a matching from C_i to $\psi(C_i)$ for a connected component $G_i = (C_i \cup \psi(C_i), E_i)$ with the vertex set $C_i \cup \psi(C_i)$. The statement of the theorem clearly holds when $|C_i| = 1$. Suppose that for all C_is with $C_i \leq \psi(C_i)$ and $|C_i| \leq m (m \geq 1)$ there exists a matching from C_i to $\psi(C_i)$ and let $m + 1 = |C_i| \leq |\psi(C_i)|$.

(1) The case where there exists a vertex v of degree 1 in $\psi(C_i)$. Since $2 \leq |C_i|$, for $w \in C_i$ such that $(w, v) \in E_i$, $deg(w) = 2$. Let $C'_i = C_i - \{w\}$. Then $\psi(C'_i) = \psi(C_i) - \{v\}$ and $G'_i = (C'_i \cup \psi(C'_i), E_i - \{(w, v)\})$ is also connected,

and $|\psi(C_i')| = |\psi(C_i)| - 1 \geq m = |C_i'|$. By the hypothesis of induction, there exists a matching M' from C_i' to $\psi(C_i')$. Adding the edge (w, v) to M', a matching from C_i to $\psi(C_i)$ is derived.

(2) The case where the degree of any vertex in $\psi(C_i)$ is equal to or greater than two, that is, there is no vertex of degree 1 in $\psi(C_i)$. Then,

(i) Since the degree of any vertex in C_i is equal to or less than two, $2 \times |\psi(C_i)| \leq |E_i| \leq 2 \times |C_i|$, which implies that $|C_i| = |\psi(C_i)|$.

(ii) Suppose that there would exist a vertex of degree 1 in C_i. Then, $2 \times |\psi(C_i)| \leq E_i < 2 \times |C_i|$, which implies that $|\psi(C_i)| < |C_i|$. This is a contraction. Therefore, the degrees of all the vertices in C_i and $\psi(C_i)$ are 2.

(iii) From (i) and (ii), a closed circuit is derived in which the vertices in C_i and $\psi(C_i)$ appear alternatively. This implies that there exist just two different matchings. (In case of a compensation graph, it can easily be shown that $|C_i|(= |\psi(C_i)|)$ for such a closed circuit is even and greater than or equal to 4.)

The theorem has been proved from (1) and (2).   □

We can judge whether a PA with faulty PEs is repairable using Theorem 2.1. On the other hand, we give a theorem below by which a matching is obtained more easily than by Theorem A in using hardware, The theorem is described in a convenient form to restructure a PA with faulty PEs, which will be used in the algorithm RA-DG-DR to be presented later.

Theorem 2.2 (Repairability theorem B)

(i) *For any vertex v of degree 1 in V_2 and $(w, v) \in E$, let $G'=(V', E')$ be the graph obtained by removing $\{w, v\}$ from V and the edges incident to w or v. Then, there exists a matching from V_1 to V_2 in G if and only if there exists a matching from $V_1 - \{w\}(=V_1')$ to $V_2 - \{v\}(=V_2')$ in G'.*

(ii) *Let the degree of any vertex in $\psi(C_i)$ be equal to or greater than two. Then,*

1. *For some C_i, if there is a vertex in $\psi(C_i)$ whose degree is greater than two, there exists no matching from V_1 to V_2.*
2. *For some C_i, if the degree of every vertex in $\psi(C_i)$ is two and there exists a vertex of degree 1 in C_i, there exists no matching from V_1 to V_2.*
3. *For all C_is, if the degree of every vertex in $\psi(C_i)$ is two and there exists no vertex of degree 1 in C_i, there exists a matching from V_1 to V_2.*

Proof *1, 2, and 3 will be proved from the following (1), (2), and (3) with Theorem 2.1, respectively.*

1. Since $2|\psi(C_i)| < |E_i| \leq 2|C_i|$, $|\psi(C_i)| < |C_i|$.

2. $|E_i| = 2|\psi(C_i)| < 2|C_i|$.

3. Since degree of every vertex in C_i is two, $2|C_i| = 2|\psi(C_i)|$.

Then, the statement is proved from the considerations 1, 2, 3, and Theorem 2.1.

                                                                                  □

The following is an algorithm for direct replacement by spare on diagonal (**RA-DG-DR**) which decides healthy spares to replace faulty PEs in terms of graph theory.

Restructuring algorithm (RA-DG-DR)

- P is a fault pattern (including faulty spares) with size of $N \times N$.
- M is a variable implying a set.

Step 1 Construct the compensation graph $G_P = (V_f \cup V_s, E)$ for P.

Step 2 Set $V_1 = V_f$, $V_2 = V_s$, and $E_1 = E$.

Step 3 Set M to an empty set ϕ. .

Step 4 While there is a vertex u with $deg(u) = 1$ in V_2, do.
For $(w, u) \in E$, set M to $M \cup \{(w, u)\}$, for $\hat{E} = \{(w, \hat{u})|(w, \hat{u})$ in E$\}$, set E to $E - \hat{E}$, $V_1 = V_1 - \{w\}$ and $V_2 = V_2 - \{u\}$ (i.e., match w with u, and delete all the edges incident to w together with w and u).

Step 5 If $V_1 = \phi$, M is a matching from V_f to V_s and go to Step 8.

Step 6 If there is a vertex in V_2 whose degree is more than 2 or there is a vertex in V_1 whose $deg(w)$ is 1, it is judged that there is no matching and go to Step 8.

Step 7 Let $\hat{G}$ be the compensation graph derived. Then, there is a matching in $\hat{G}$ and find a closed cycle in each derived connected component $\hat{C}_i$, from which just two different matching in $\hat{C}_i$ are derived. Choose one of them which is denoted as M_i. Let $M = M \cup \{\cup_i M_i\}$. Then M is a matching from V_f to V_s.

Step 8 End. □

For the example in Fig. 2.6, the four matchings $M_1,...,M_4$ are obtained. They are $M_1 = m_{11} \cup m_{21}$, $M_2 = m_{11} \cup m_{22}$, $M_3 = m_{12} \cup m_{21}$, and $M_4 = m_{12} \cup m_{22}$ where $m_{11} = \{(X_5, s_6), (X_1, s_1), (X_4, s_4)\}$, $m_{12} = \{(X_5, s_6), (X_4, s_1), (X_1, s_4)\}$, $m_{21} = \{(X_2, s_2), (X_3, s_3), (X_6, s_5)\}$, and $m_{22} = \{(X_2, s_2), (X_3, s_5), (X_6, s_3)\}$,

In the following, we will describe how to realize RA-DG-DR by hardware. To do so, it is sufficient to make circuits by which Steps 4, 6, and 7 are executed. So, first, we will give an interconnection structure which is shown in Fig. 2.7 where in addition, two faulty PEs are shown with the mark X's and the replaced directions. The switches around a PE consist of H- and V-switches whose are denoted as H-sw and V-sw. The states of the switches are determined as in Fig. 2.8, depending on whether the PE is healthy or faulty and the directions in which it is replaced by a spare.

2.2.2 Hardware Realization of the Algorithm

By the way, as a preparation for showing circuits to realize RA-DG-DR, we will show how to get the number of faults to be replaced for each spare using the example shown in Fig. 2.6.

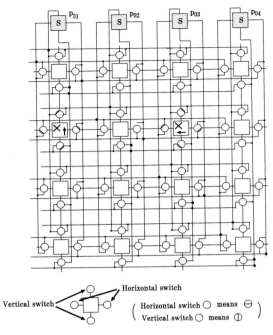

Fig. 2.7   An interconnection structure where spare PEs are physically located on the upper side, but logically on the diagonal

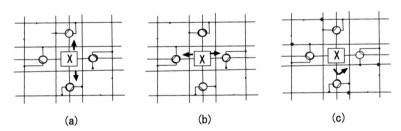

Fig. 2.8   The states of switches around PE according to the directions in which it is replaced, **a** upward or downward (UD-state), **b** rightward or leftward (RL-state), and **c** ON-ward (J-state), i.e., faulty PE is on the diagonal

Figure 2.9 is the fault pattern where "0" or "1" denotes the fault state of PE (if PE is faulty, 1, otherwise 0). Note that the spares are in the top row.

Figure 2.10 shows how to get the number of faults (denoted as $n_f(S_i)$) to be replaced by each spare S_i. It is obtained by adding the number of faults on the horizontal and vertical lines through each spare S_i as shown in Fig. 2.10 (in which the row together with column is denoted as $RC(S_i)$). From the figure, it is seen that $n_f(S_i)$'s $(1 \leq i \leq 6)$ are 2, 1, 2, 3, 3, and 1, respectively. Note that $n_f(S_i)$ is equal to the degree of the vertex s_i of S_i.

Fig. 2.9 A fault pattern in
Fig. 2.6

$$
\begin{array}{cccccc}
0 & 0 & 0 & 0 & 0 & 0 \\
0 & 0 & 0 & 1 & 0 & 0 \\
0 & 0 & 0 & 0 & 1 & 0 \\
0 & 0 & 0 & 0 & 1 & 0 \\
1 & 0 & 0 & 0 & 0 & 1 \\
0 & 0 & 1 & 0 & 0 & 0 \\
0 & 0 & 0 & 0 & 0 & 0 \\
\end{array}
$$

Fig. 2.10 The numbers of
faults $n_f(S_i)$'s

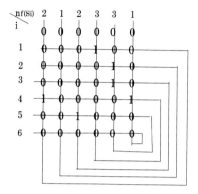

The following is the detailed process for applying RA-DG-DR to PA, where spare
PEs are physically located on the upper side as shown in Fig. 2.7.

Restructuring algorithm (RA-DG-DR(PA))

- Input PA with size of $N \times N$

Step 1 While there is an unrepaired faulty PE in RC(S_j) with $n_f(S_j)=1$ for some
S_j, do (i) below.
(i) For each spare S_j, get $n_f(S_j)$. This is done in parallel for all the spares
S_j's. Then, replace (repair) a faulty PE in RC(S_j) with $n_f(S_j)=1$ by the spare
S_j, set $n_f(S_j)$ to 0 and the fault state of the faulty PE to 0.
This step corresponds to Step 4 in RA-DG-DR.

Step 2 For some S_j, if $n_f(S_j) \geq 3$ or (for $n_f(S_j) = 2$, S_j or the nonspare PE at the
location of S_j is faulty and unrepaired), the PA with faults is unrepairable
and go to Step 4.
This step corresponds to Step 6 in RA-DG-DR.

Step 3 The array is repairable. Then, proceed to find closed cycles and determine
the directions of replacement for the unrepaired faulty PEs in the cycles.
This step corresponds to Step 7 in RA-DG-DR.

Step 4 The algorithm ends. ☐

RA-DG-DR(PA) will be realized by digital circuits for the interconnection structure shown in Fig. 2.7. This is done by two circuits similarly as in Sect. 3.3. Hence,
they are not described here.

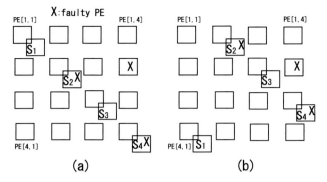

(a)   (b)

Fig. 2.11 Given fault pattern is **a** unrepairable in the diagonal defined until now, **b** repairable in moved diagonal

2.2.3 Moving Diagonal Method

Figure 2.11 is an example of a fault pattern which is unrepairable in (a) the diagonal defined until now, but repairable in (b) the moved diagonal, where faulty PE(2, 4) marked with X is unrepairable in (a) but repairable by spare S_3 in (b). This suggests that moving diagonal may increase the array reliabilities.

From the above, the following algorithm is proposed for an $N \times N$ array.

Noting that a diagonal is defined if the spare $S(k)$ is specified in the first row, PA with such diagonal is denoted as PA(k).

Diagonal moving algorithm (RA-MDG-DR(PA))

Input: A fault pattern P.

Step 1. Set *sfg* to 1 and k to 0.
Step 2. Increase k by 1.
Step 3. Apply RA-DG-DR to PA(k).
Step 4. If *sfg*=0 and $k < N$, goto Step 2.
Step 5. If *sfg*=0, P is unrepairable. Otherwise, repairable.   □
Step 6. End

Hardware realization of RA-MDG-DR(PA)

By adding four switches around each PE shown in Fig. 2.7, it could be checked that each spare will be logically allocated at arbitrary row. Using the property, the diagonal can be moved as intended. The details of this and the others should be referred to [1].

2.3 Spares on Diagonal with Single-Track-Shift Replacement (DG-STS)

DG-DR scheme achieves higher survival rates than DG-STS scheme. On the other hand, DG-DR scheme has a disadvantage in that physical distances among logically adjacent PEs after restructuring are proportional to the array sizes. So, we will introduce DG-STS scheme which replaces a faulty PE by shifting PEs as in [2], which is called STS method. DG-STS scheme has an advantage in that physical distances among logically adjacent PEs after restructuring are bounded by a constant though the survival rates obtained by DG-STS scheme are lower than those by DG-DR scheme.[1]

2.3.1 Restructuring Algorithm (RA-DG-STS)

The restructuring using STS method is done as described in Sect. 2.1.2. That is, a faulty nonspare PE is bypassed and replaced by its adjacent healthy PE, which in turn is replaced by the next adjacent healthy PE, and so on. This replacement is repeated until a healthy spare PE is used in the end. The restructuring process defines a compensation path (c-path). In Fig. 2.12, the directions of c-paths are depicted with the arrows. Note that (i) the c-path is straight and continuous, and must not pass other faulty PEs, and (ii) two c-paths must not cross, i.e., pass must not be the same PE where if c-paths c_1 and c_2 pass the same PE as shown in Fig. 2.12, they are called to be in **intersection relation**.

Property 2.3 (Repairability condition (**RC-STS**)) *An array with faulty PEs is repairable if and only if there is a set of c-paths S which satisfies the condition*

1. *S contains a c-path for each nonspare faulty PE, and*
2. *there is no intersection among the c-paths in S.*   □

    A strategy to get a set of c-paths S for an array with a fault pattern, which satisfies RC-STS, could be formalized as matching and independent problems in graph theory.

Fig. 2.12 C-paths c_1 and c_2 in intersection relation

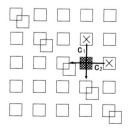

---

[1] The content in this section is written, based on the paper [3].

Fig. 2.13 Left and right
triangle subarrays

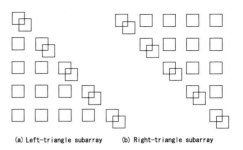

(a) Left-triangle subarray   (b) Right-triangle subarray

However, it seems to be difficult to realize the strategy in hardware, that is, a built-in
self-repairing system. Hence, we present another method to be given by an algorithm
RA-DG-STS as follows.

RA-DG-STS consists of Right-RA and Left-RA shown below. Given an array,
first, two triangle subarrays are made as shown in Fig. 2.13 in which PEs and spares on
the diagonal overlap between two subarrays. They are often called the right- and left-
triangle subarrays, and denoted as RT- and LT-subarrays, respectively. Then, Right-
RA is applied to the RT-subarray with spares to compensate for faults in it. Next, Left-
RA is applied to the LT-subarray with spares not used in Right-RA to compensate for
faults in the LT-subarray. Note that Left-RA is obtained by exchanging the variables
i and j in Right-RA with small modifications, and so, not described in detail.

Restructuring algorithm (RA-DG-STS)

- A matrix $P = (p_{ij})$ $(1 \le i \le N, 0 \le j \le N)$ is a fault pattern.
- $D = (d_{ij})$ is a matrix with the same size as that of P.
- *flg* and *sfg* are flags.

Input: a fault pattern $P = (p_{ij})$.
Output: the value of *sfg* where *sfg*=1 (=0) means that P is repairable (unrepairable).

Right-RA

Do the following Steps
   Step 1. Set the values of all the elements in D to 0s and *sfg* to 1.
Step 2. Decreasing the variable j from N to 1, do
   Step 2-1. Set *flg* to s_j.
   Step 2-2. decreasing the variable i from j to 1, do
      Step 2-2-1. If $d_{ij}=2$, then set *flg* to 1.
      Step 2-2-2. If $(p_{ij}=1$ and *flg*=1), do
         Step 2-2-2-1. if $i = j$, set *sfg* to 0, and goto Step 3
         Step 2-2-2-2. else do
         Step 2-2-2-3. set d_{ij} to 2.
         Step 2-2-2-4. decreasing k from j-1 to i, do
         Step 2-2-2-5. if (s_1=1 or p_{ik}=1), set *sfg* to 0, and finish the algorithm.

Step 2-2-2-6. else set d_{ik} to 2 and

(9-a)   set s_i to 1. (Note 1)

Step 2-2-3. If ($p_{ij}=1$ and $flg=0$), then do

Step 2-2-3-1. set flg to 1,

Step 2-2-3-2. decreasing k from i to j, then do

Step 2-2-3-3. set d_{kj} to 1.

(11-a)   Step 2-2-3-4. set s_j to 1. (Note 2)

(11-b)   Step 2-2-3-5. set p_{jj} to 0. (Note 3)

Step 3. The algorithm ends.

Note 1: Since $S(i)$ has been used to compensate for the faulty PE(i, j), s_i is set to 1 so that $S(i)$ should not be used in Left-RA.

Note 2: Since $S(j)$ has been used to compensate for a faulty PE(i, j), s_j is set to 1 so that $S(j)$ should not be used in Left-RA.

Note 3: Since if $i = j$, PE(j, j) is compensated for, otherwise PE(i, j) is healthy, p_{jj} is set to 0 so that PE(j, j) can be accessed in Left-RA.

Left-RA

This is derived by exchanging the row and column indices in Right-RA without the processes (9-a), (11-a) and (11-b)

□

The process in Right-RA is outlined as follows.

1. At start, the rightmost column, i.e., the N-th column is scanned upward from the spare PE on the diagonal, Then if a faulty PE is met without meeting other faulty PE, the downward 1-sequence (means c-path) to the spare PE on the diagonal is generated. If it is met after meeting other faulty PE, the leftward 2-sequence (means c-path) to the spare on the diagonal is generated.
2. If the above processes are successful for all PEs on the column, that is, $sfg=1$, the similar processes are executed on the column next to the left, and so on.
3. If the above processes are at last successfully executed on the left-most column, Right-RA ends with $sfg=1$ and the fault pattern in the RT-subarray is judged to be repairable. Then, faulty PEs with downward (leftward) c-path is repaired by downward (leftward) shift.
4. Otherwise, the algorithm ends with $sfg=0$ and the fault pattern in the RT-subarray as well as the array is judged to be unrepairable.
5. If the process in Right-RA ends successfully, i.e., $sfg=1$, the process in Left-RA is executed as in Right-RA, where it starts from the N-th row toward the 1-st row and 1-seq's (2-seq's) are generated rightward (upward),

Figure 2.14 illustrates a fault pattern with the process executed in Right-RA and Left-RA.

Then, the following properties for repairability are given, where only the proof of Property 2.4 will be described but the proofs of the others will be omitted.

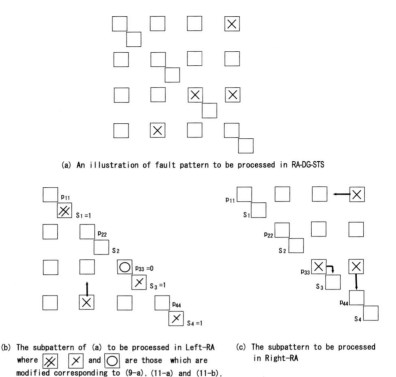

(a) An illustration of fault pattern to be processed in RA-DG-STS

(b) The subpattern of (a) to be processed in Left–RA
where $\boxtimes$, $\times$ and $\bigcirc$ are those which are
modified corresponding to (9–a), (11–a) and (11–b),
respectively

(c) The subpattern to be processed
in Right–RA

Fig. 2.14   An illustration of a fault pattern where arrow lines indicate the directions of c-paths. **c** is
the right subpattern to be processed in Right-RA. **b** is the left subpattern to be processed in Left-RA

Property 2.4 (**Right-repairability**) *A fault pattern in an RT-subarray is repairable
(in the meaning of Property 2.3) if and only if Right-RA ends with sfg=1. If it ends
with sfg=1, the set of 1- and 2-sequences is a set of c-paths which satisfies RC-STS
described in Property 2.3.*   □

Proof See Appendix A.

Property 2.5

1. *An array with a fault pattern is repairable if RA-DG-STS applied to the fault
   pattern ends with sfg=1. If ends with sfg=1, the set of 1- and 2-sequences is a
   set of c-paths which satisfies the condition in Property 2.3.*
2. *If Right-RA applied to a fault pattern ends with sfg=0, there is no set of c-paths
   for the array with the fault pattern which satisfies the condition in Property 2.3.*
                                                                                      □

Fig. 2.15 Interconnection structure for DG-STS scheme and an illustration of states of switches to compensate for a fault pattern where × s denote faulty PEs. The arrows show the directions of c-paths for faulty PEs

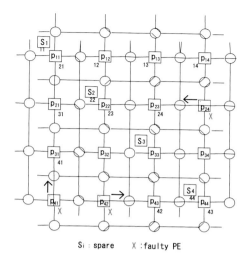

S_i : spare   X :faulty PE

2.3.2 Hardware Realization of the Algorithm

In a hardware realization of DG-STS scheme, how to locate spare PEs should be considered. So, first, we show an interconnection structure for DG-STS scheme in Fig. 2.15. A single track runs between adjacent rows and between adjacent columns, and there is a switch at the cross of a track and a link around each PE. Figure 2.16 shows the states of sw's around a healthy (faulty) PE. Figures 2.17 and 2.18 show the states of sw's around a PE on the diagonal according to the directions of c-paths.

Figure 2.19 shows a hardware realization of RA-DG-STS, together with an illustration of signals in CC-net. Each PE has a logical circuit CC, which is connected as shown in Fig. 2.19. CC has four input signals p, D_{in}, L_{in}, and U_{in} and four output signals D_{out}, L_{out}, U_{out}, and S_{fg} ($=\overline{S_{fg}^{nd}}$ or $\overline{S_{fg}^{d}}$). As to be described later, D_{in} corresponds to flg, L_{out} to 2-sequence, U_{out} to 1-sequence, respectively, and the logical AND of S_{fg}'s from all CC's corresponds to sfg.

Fig. 2.16 SWs are switched as in **a** and **b** according to whether PE is healthy and faulty, respectively

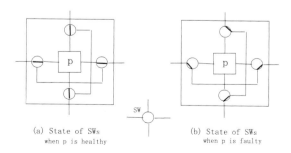

(a) State of SWs when p is healthy

(b) State of SWs when p is faulty

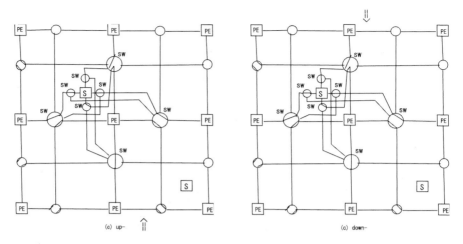

Fig. 2.17 States of the switches on the diagonal for up- and down-directional c-paths whose directions are shown as arrows, respectively

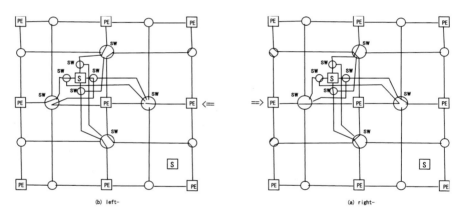

Fig. 2.18 States of the switches on the diagonal for left- and right-directional c-paths whose directions are shown as arrows, respectively

Considering correspondence among the variables in RA-DG-STS and the signals in CCs, we have the following logical equations.

$$D_{out} = p + D_{in} + L_{in} \tag{2.1}$$

$$L_{out} = L_{in} + p \cdot D_{in} \tag{2.2}$$

$$U_{out} = U_{in} + p \cdot \overline{D_{in}} \tag{2.3}$$

$$\overline{S_{fg}^{nd}} = p \cdot L_{in} \tag{2.4}$$

$$\overline{S_{fg}^{d}} = p \cdot (L_{in} + D_{in}) + L_{in} \cdot D_{in} \tag{2.5}$$

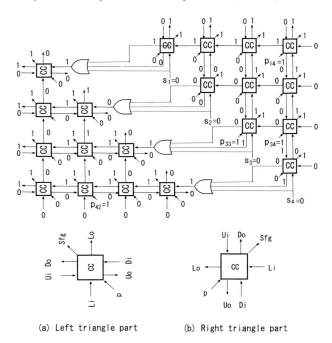

(a) Left triangle part   (b) Right triangle part

Fig. 2.19   An illustration of signals in CC-net for a 4 × 4 array with faults shown in Fig. 2.14

$\overline{S_{fg}^{nd}}$ and $\overline{S_{fg}^{d}}$ are for CC which is "not on" and "on" the diagonal, respectively.

Note that from the equations above, the logical circuit CC is so simple and no flip-flop is used.

Then, the behavior of CC-net shown in Fig. 2.19 is compatible with that of RA-DG-STS, which is shown from Properties 2.8, 2.9 and 2.10. Property 2.8 is used to check whether an array with faulty PE's is repairable or not. Property 2.9 shows the correspondence between 2-sequences and sequences of L_{out}'s. Property 2.10 shows the correspondence between 1-sequences and sequences of U_{out}'s.

By the way, since the CC-net shown in Fig. 2.19b behaves in asynchronous mode, we will prove that the signals in the network become stable for any fixed inputs.

For convenience of explanation, the terminal names and the signals from/in the terminals are often identically used unless confused, and the signals from/in CC of PE(x, y) are denoted with index "(x, y)".

Note that $L_{in}(x, N) = 0$ for any x ($1 \leq x \leq N$) and $U_{in}(1, y) = 0$ for any y ($1 \leq y \leq N$). Further, let $L_{in}(y + 1, y)=D_{in}(y + 1, y) = 0$ and $p_{y+1y}=s_y$. Then, $D_{out}(y + 1, y)=D_{in}(y, y)=s_y$.

Lemma 2.1   *Let t_d denote signal propagation time in CC. For any column of CC's whose size is $k \times 1$, the signals in the column become stable within $(2k - 1) \cdot t_d$ after external inputs to the column are fixed.*

Proof *Note that the external inputs to the y-th column are $D_{in}(y, y)(= s_y)$, $L_{in}(x, y)(1 \leq x \leq y)$, $p_{xy}(1 \leq x \leq y)$ and $U_{in}(1, y)$, and the outputs from the y-th column go to the left, but not to the right. Now, let the external inputs to the column be fixed. We will prove by induction on k. The statement clearly holds for the case of $k = 1$. Let $k \geq 2$. Since from Eq. (2.1) $D_{out}(k, k)$ depends only on the external inputs $D_{in}(k, k)(= s_k)$, p_{kk} and $L_{in}(k, k)$ inputs, $D_{in}(k - 1, k)$ $(=D_{out}(k, k))$ becomes stable in t_d. Then, since the inputs to CC's on the k-th column which consists of rows except the k-th row are fixed, from the hypothesis of induction the signals in all CC's on k-th column become stable within $(2(k - 1) - 1) \cdot t_d$. After that, since $U_{in}(k, y) = U_{out}(k - 1, y)$, $U_{out}(k, y)$ is fixed in t_d. In total, the signals become stable within $(2k - 1) \cdot t_d$.* □

Since external signals on a column come from its right neighbors, we have the following property.

Property 2.6 *For the CC-net for the RT-subarray of an array of logical size $N \times N$, the signals become stable within $N^2 \cdot t_d$ for any fault pattern.* □

In the following, from Property 2.6 we assume that the signals have become stable. Then, we show the following properties which are closely related to hardware realization of RA-DG-STS . Their proofs are omitted since they are long and tedious.

Property 2.7 *The RT-subarray of an array with a fault pattern is repairable if and only if all the output signals S_{fg}'s from CC's are 1's.*

□

Property 2.8 *An array with a fault pattern is repairable if all the output signals S_{fg}'s from CC's in both RT- and LT-subarrays are 1's.*

□

Now, we discuss how to switch the connections among PE's if the logical AND of all the output signals S_{fg}'s from CC's is 1. Hence, in the following, we assume that a repairable fault pattern is given, that is, the logical AND of all the output signals S_{fg}'s from CC's is 1. In order to switch the connections among PE's correctly, from Property 2.4 it is necessary and sufficient to know the correspondences between 1- or 2-sequences in RA-DG-STS and the signals in the CC-net. Such correspondences are given by the following properties.

Property 2.9 $d_{xy} = 2$ *if and only if $L_{out}(x, y) = 1$.* □

Property 2.10 $d_{xy} = 1$ *if and only if $U_{out}(x, y) = 1$.* □

From the above, there are one-to-one correspondences between 1-sequences and sequences of U_{out}'s, and between 2-sequences and sequences of L_{out}'s. Then, from Property 2.4 we could give a truth table defining the states of switches, using U_{out}'s and L_{out}'s. However, it will be omitted since it is not so difficult task.

Figure 2.19 illustrates signals in CC-net for a 4×4 array with the faults shown in Fig. 2.14. The signal 1 from L_{out} of $CC(1, 1)$ in the right triangle part to the

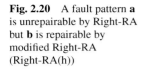

Fig. 2.20   A fault pattern **a** is unrepairable by Right-RA but **b** is repairable by modified Right-RA (Right-RA(h))

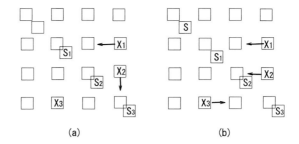

(a)   (b)

OR-gate connected to D_i of $CC(1, 1)$ in the left triangle part corresponds to (9-a) in Right-RA. Similarly, 1's from U_{out} of $CC(3, 3)$ in the right triangle part to the OR-gate connected to D_i of $CC(3, 3)$ in the left triangle part and from that of U_{out} of $CC(4, 4)$ to L_{in} of $CC(4, 4)$ correspond to (11-a) in Right-RA. $p_{33} = 0$ of $CC(3, 3)$ in the left triangle part instead of $p_{33} = 1$ in the right triangle part corresponds to (11-b).

By the way, as to be shown in Fig. 2.20, Property 2.8 has given a sufficient but not necessary condition that an array with a fault pattern is repairable. It is hoped that a necessary and sufficient condition will be given to achieve the highest reliability in the DG scheme using STS method. However, even if it would be given, it seems that the hardware realization, that is, a built-in circuit for it, will become complicated. So, here we present an extended algorithm to achieve higher reliability as Right-RA(h). It is the modification of Right-RA where i and j in Right-RA are exchanged and small changes are made according to the exchange. The modified parts are as follows.

Modifying Right-RA to Right-RA(h)

1. Exchanged i and j.
2. Step 2 in Right-RA is changed to "Increasing the variable i from 1 to N, do"
3. Step 2-1 is to "Set flg to s_i".
4. Step 2-2 is to "Increasing i from 1 to N".
5. Step 2-2-2-4 is to increasing the value k from $i + 1$ to j, do".
6. Step 2-2-2-5 is to "if ($s_j = 1$ or $p_{kj} = 1$) then".
7. Step 2-2-2-6 is to "else set d_{kj} to 2".
8. Step 2-2-3-3 is to "set d_{ik} to 1;"   □

From the similarity between Right-RA and Right-RA(h), we have the following property.

Property 2.11 *Right-RA(h) ends with sfg=1 if and only if Right-RA ends with sfg=1.*   □

Then, the extended algorithm RA-DG-STS-ex is as follows.

RA-DG-STS-ex

Step 1 Execute Right-RA in RA-DG-STS . If it ends with *sfg*=1, goto Step 3.

Step 2 else it ends with $sfg=0$. The given fault pattern is unrepairable and goto Step 6

Step 3 Execute Left-RA. If it ends with $sfg=1$, the fault pattern is judged to be repairable and goto Step 6

Step 4 Execute Right-RA(h) followed by Left-RA. If it ends with $sfg=1$, the fault pattern is judged to be repairable and goto Step 6

Step 5 (else it ends with $sfg=0$) The fault pattern is judged to be unrepairable.

Step 6 The algorithm ends.   □

Now, we describe a hardware realization of RA-DG-STS-ex. CC for Right-RA shown in Fig. 2.21a are the same as those in the right triangle part in Fig. 2.19b. CC for Right-RA(h) shown in Fig. 2.21b is that for CC in (a) turned clockwise by 90 degrees, and L_i and L_o are exchanged. Then, Fig. 2.21a, b are realized as shown in Figs. 2.22 and 2.23, by only switching sw's around CC, respectively.

2.4 Survival Rates and Array Reliabilities

We estimate the performance of the algorithms mentioned in this section in terms of the survival rate (SV) and array reliability ($AR(p)$) which are defined below. $AR(p)$ is the sum of all the probabilities each of which is computed as the product of probability that a fault pattern is repaired and one that the pattern occurs under the condition that each PE may be healthy with equal probability p.

Notation 2.4

- N_s is the number of spare PEs.
- $N_{rep}(k)$ is the number of fault patterns which have k faulty PEs and are judged to be repairable.
- $N_{pat}(k)$ is the number of examined fault patterns which have k faulty PEs.
- N_a is the number of all PEs.   □

$$SV(k) = \frac{N_{rep}(k)}{N_{pat}(k)},$$

$$AR(p) = \sum_{k=0}^{N_s} {}_{Na}C_k \cdot SV(k) \cdot p^{N_a-k} \cdot (1-p)^k,$$

Fig. 2.21 **a** CC's in the hardware realization of Right RA. **b** CC's in that of Right-RA(h)

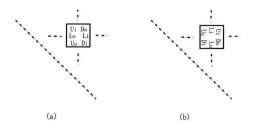

(a)   (b)

Fig. 2.22 State of sw's in CC's on executing Right-RA in RA-DG-STS -ex

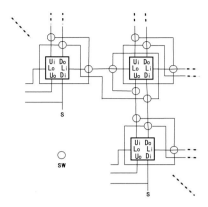

Note that $p^{N_a-k} \cdot (1-p)^k$ is the probability that a fault pattern with k faulty PEs occurs, $_{N_a}C_k = \frac{N_a!}{(N_a-k)!k!}$ the number of fault patterns each with k faulty PEs, $SV(k)$ so called the survival rate which is the ratio of the number of repairable fault patterns each with k faulty PEs and the number of fault patterns each with k faulty PEs examined, which is the probability estimated by simulation that fault patterns each with k faulty PEs are repaired.

Monte Carlo simulations, using a PC machine with Borland C++Compiler 5.5, are executed under the condition that all the PEs may become uniformly faulty. Then, 10^6 random fault patterns each with k faulty PEs for $1 \leq k \leq N_s$ are generated.

From Fig. 2.24, it is seen that the AR obtained by RA-DG-STS-ex increases, comparing with that by RA-DG-STS.

Figure 2.25a shows the survival rates (SVs) of arrays with size of 8×8, where "-mov" denotes one for RA-MDG-DR, "-fix" for RA-MDG-DR with diagonal fixed and -STS for STS method, respectively and (b) shows the array reliabilities (ARs) with size of 8×8 where -ss denotes AR for ss-scheme (Fig. 2.26).

Fig. 2.23 State of sw's in CC's on executing Right-RA(h) in RA-DG-STS -ex

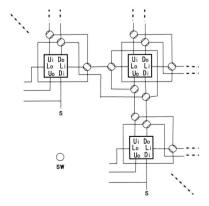

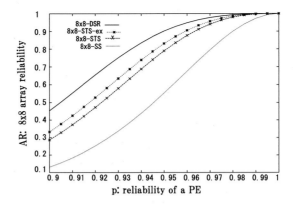

Fig. 2.24   AR versus p for 8×8 arrays

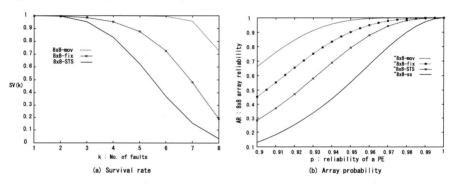

Fig. 2.25 a Survival rates and **b** array reliabilities for 8×8 arrays

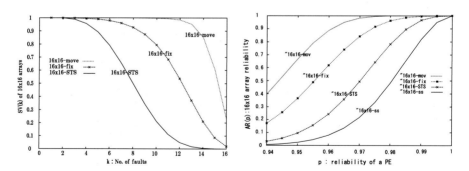

Fig. 2.26 a Survival rates and **b** array reliabilities for 16×16 arrays

It is seen that the ARs and survival rates for RA-MDG-DR are much higher than those for STS as well as the fixed RA-MDG-DR for PA(1).

Appendix A: The proof of Property 2.4

Property 2.4 is proved by a sequence of the following Proposition and Lemmas.

Proposition 2.1 *In processing a column of an array, if flg changes from 0 to 1 at a row, it does not change from 1 to 0 at the succeeding rows. sfg=1 at the beginning of a process, and the process ends with sfg=0 if sfg changes from 1 to 0, otherwise with sfg=1.*

Proof This is easily shown from Right-RA.   □

Notation 2.5 1. The statements of Steps 2 and 2-2 are also expressed as "for $j=N$ to 1" and "$i=j$ to 1", respectively and called "for-statement". Then, the process that "for-statement" at $j = j_0$ $(1 \leq j_0 \leq N)$ and $i = i_0$ $(1 \leq i_0 \leq j)$ in Right-RA is executed is denoted as "for-process at (i_0, j_0)".
2. $flg_{i_0 j_0}$ $(1 \leq i_0 \leq j_0)$ denotes the value of flg just after for-process at (i_0, j_0) is executed.
3. $d_{i_0 j_0}$s denote the values after Right-RA has been executed.   □

Lemma 2.2 *For any j $(N \geq j \geq 1)$ and any i $(j \geq i \geq 1)$, $flg_{ij} = 1$ if and only if $s_j = 1$, $p_{\hat{i} j} = 1$ or $d_{\hat{i} j} = 2$ for some $\hat{i}$ $(j \geq \hat{i} \geq i \geq 1)$.*

Proof From Right-RA, the following is easily seen. If $flg_{ij} = 0$, $flg_{i' j} = 0$ for any $i' \geq i$. Then $s_j = 0$, $p_{i' j} = 0$ and $d_{i' j} = 0$ for any $i' \geq i$. If $s_j = 0$, $p_{i' j} = 0$ and $d_{i' j} = 0$ for any $i' \geq i$, $flg_{i' j} = 0$ for any $i' \geq i$.

                                                                                          □

Lemma 2.3 *(i) 1-seq(i, j) never passes other faulty PEs than PE(i, j).*
(ii) 2-seq(i, j) never passes other faulty PEs than PE(i, j).

Proof (i) 1-seq(i, j) is generated downward at Step 2-2-3-3 in for-process at (i, j) from a faulty PE(i, j). Hence, $p_{ij}=1$ and $flg_{(i+1)j}=0$. Therefore, from Lemma 2.2 $p_{\hat{i} j}=0$ for all $\hat{i}$ $(j \geq \hat{i} \geq i + 1)$ and $s_j=0$, and this means that the 1-seq(i, j) never passes other faulty PEs (including the spare $S(j)$) than PE(i, j).

        (ii) Since a 2-sequence is generated at Step 2-2-2-3 and 2-2-2-6 in for-process at (i, j) from a faulty PE(i, j), and it reaches a spare, it is clear that it never passes other faulty PEs than PE(i, j).   □

Lemma 2.4 *2-sequences neither intersect nor overlap each other.*

Proof It is clear that they never intersect since they go only in the left direction. We suppose that there exist 2-seq(i, j) and 2-seq(i', j') $((i, j) \neq (i', j'))$ which overlap. Then $p_{ij} = p_{i' j'} = 1$ and $i = i'$. Without loss of generality, it can be assumed that $j' > j$. Then sfg becomes 0 at Step 2-2-2-5 in for-process at (i, j') and a sequence of 2's from PE(i, j') can't reach the spare $S(i)$. This contradicts that there exist 2-seq(i, j) and 2-seq(i', j') which overlap.   □

Lemma 2.5 *1-sequences neither intersect nor overlap each other. Furthermore, 1-sequences and 2-sequences never intersect each other.*

Proof It is clear that no 1-sequences intersect each other since they go only downward. We suppose that there exist 1-seq(i, j) and 1-seq(i', j') $((i, j) \neq (i', j'))$ which overlap. Then $p_{ij} = p_{i'j'} = 1$ and $j = j'$ since a 1-sequence is generated at Step 2-2-3-3. Without loss of generality, $i' > i$ can be assumed. Then 1-seq(i, j) passes the faulty PE(i', j'), which contradicts Lemma 2.3. Next, we suppose that there exist 1-seq(i, j) and 2-seq(i', j') which intersect. Then $i' \geq i$ and $j' \geq j$, and from the flow of execution in Right-RA 1-seq(i, j) is generated after 2-seq(i', j') is generated. If $i = i'$, 2-seq(i', j') passes the faulty PE(i, j), which contradicts Lemma 2.3. If $i' > i$, the process Step 2-2-1 in for-process at (i', j) is executed since $d_{i'j} = 2$, and $flg_{i'j} = 1$. Hence, from Proposition 2.1, $flg_{ij} = 1$. Therefore, the process Step 2-2-3-1 is not executed in for-process at (i, j), and 1-seq(i, j) is not generated. This contradicts that there exist 1-seq(i, j) and 1-seq(i', j') $((i, j) \neq (i', j'))$ which overlap.   □

Lemma 2.6 *Let $p_{ij} = 1$, that is, PE(i, j) be faulty. If $flg_{(i+1)j} = 1$, the downward c-path (if it exists) from PE(i, j) is not included in any set of c-paths which satisfies RC-STS described in Property 2.3.*

Proof Let $p_{ij} = flg_{(i+1)j} = 1$. Then, from Lemma 2.2 $s_j = 1$, $p_{\hat{i}j} = 1$, or $d_{\hat{i}j} = 2$ for some $\hat{i}$ $(j \geq \hat{i} \geq i + 1)$. We will prove by induction on the number of 2-sequences t. If $t = 0$, no d_{uv} is 2 and hence, $s_j = 1$ or $p_{\hat{i}j} = 1$ for some $\hat{i}$ $(j \geq \hat{i} \geq i + 1)$, and it is clear that there is not a downward c-path from PE(i, j).

Let $t \geq 1$. For the case where $s_j = 1$ or $p_{\hat{i}j} = 1$ for some $\hat{i}$ $(j \geq \hat{i} \geq i + 1)$, the proof is similar as above. Otherwise, $s_j = 0$ and $p_{i'j} = 0$ for any i' $(j \geq i' \geq i + 1)$ and $d_{\hat{i}j} = 2$ for some $\hat{i}$ $(j \geq \hat{i} \geq i + 1)$. Then there exists 2-seq$(\hat{i}, j')$ for some j' $(j' \geq j)$. Just before the 2-seq$(\hat{i}, j')$ is generated at Step 2-2-2 to 2-2-2-6 in for-process$(\hat{i}, j')$, the number of 2-sequences is less than t, and $d_{\hat{i}j'} = 0$, $p_{\hat{i}j'} = 1$ and $flg_{\hat{i}j'} = 1$. Therefore, since Step 2-2-1 is not executed but Step 2-2-2 is executed, $flg_{\hat{i}+1j'} = 1$, and from the hypothesis of induction, the downward c-path (if it exists) from PE$(\hat{i}, j')$ is not included in any set of c-paths which satisfies RC-STS. This implies that a c-path from faulty PE$(\hat{i}, j')$ must be taken in the left direction. However, the downward c-path from PE(i, j) intersects the left-directional c-path from PE$(\hat{i}, j')$. This implies that the downward c-path (if it exists) from PE(i, j) is not included in any set of c-paths which satisfies RC-STS.   □

The proof of Property 3.11. (**"only if" part**): We assume that the algorithm ends with $sfg = 0$ and suppose that there exists a set S of c-paths which satisfies RC-STS. sfg becomes 0 at Step 2-2-2-1 or 2-2-2-5 in for-process at some (i, j). Then $p_{ij} = 1$ (that is, PE(i, j) is faulty) and $flg = 1$ at Step 2-2-2. If $flg_{(i+1)j} = 0$, $d_{ij} = 2$ at Step 2-2-1 and hence, a 2-seq(i, j') for some j' $(j < j')$ passes the faulty PE(i, j). This contradicts (ii) in Lemma 2.3. Therefore $flg_{(i+1)j} = 1$. Then, from Lemma 2.6, S must contain the left-directional c-path from PE(i, j). However, there exist faulty PEs in the left direction from PE(i, j) since sfg becomes 0, and hence the left-directional c-path for PE(i, j) is also not included in S. This contradicts the property of S. Therefore, there exists no set of c-paths which satisfies RC-STS.

(**'if part**): We assume that the algorithm ends with $sfg = 1$. If $flg = 1$ at Step 2-2-2 in for-process at (i, j) for $p_{ij} = 1$ (that is, PE(i, j) is faulty), the processes at Step 2-2-2-3 and 2-2-2-6 generate 2-seq(i, j) which reaches the spare on the diagonal in the left-direction from (i, j). If $flg = 0$ for $p_{ij} = 1$, the process at Step 2-2-2-3 generates 1-seq(i, j) which reaches the spare on the diagonal in the downward from (i, j). From Lemma 2.3 these sequences are c-paths from PE(i, j). Furthermore, these sequences from faulty PEs neither intersect nor overlap each other. Therefore, the set of 1- and 2-sequences obtained satisfies RC-STS.   □

References

1. Ituso, T., Masaru, F.: Self-restructuring of mesh-connected processor arrays through spares on moved diagonal, direct replacement and built-in circuits. SCIREA J. Comput. **8**(2), 91–117 (2023)
2. Kung, S.Y., Jean, S.N., Chang, C.W.: Fault-tolerant array processors using single-track switches. IEEE Trans. Comput. **38**(4), 501–514 (1989)
3. Ituso, T., Masaru, F.: A Built-in Self-repair Circuit for Self-restructuring Mesh Connected Processor Arrays with Spares on Diagonal, Trans. on Computational Science XXXIV, pp. 109–135. Springer (2019)

Chapter 3
2D Arrays with $2N$ Spares

Abstract Arrays with spares on the opposite sides (OP) and orthogonal two sides (OT) as spare arrangements are treated. Restructurings faults with spares are done by either DR or STS for each spare arrangement. Restructuring algorithms which satisfy the repairability conditions are given. Further, degradable restructuring schemes for spares on the orthogonal two sides, i.e., restructuring with deleting rows and/or columns, are described and the evaluations for them are shown. This implies the reuse of arrays with faults by decreasing the sizes of arrays.

Keywords Fault-tolerance · Two-dimensional array · Spares on opposite sides · Spares on orthogonal sides · Restructuring · Reconfiguration · Degradable restructuring · Direct replacement · Single-track shift · Built-in circuit · Spare rotation

3.1 Spares on Opposite Sides (OPSS)

Figure 3.1 shows the opposite side spare scheme (in short, written as OPSS) in which spares are located on opposite two sides of an array with size of $N \times (N + 2)$ (logical size is $N \times N$). In OPSS, a faulty PE is replaced by either of two spares on the same row. In the following, two interconnection structures are introduced. One is a structure for STS replacing method (OP-STS). Another is a structure for double track shift replacing method (OP-DTS).[1]

3.1.1 Restructuring Algorithm (RA-OP-STS)

Figure 3.2a shows an interconnection structure for OP-STS. The tracks run along toward the spares located on the opposite sides (horizontally in the figure).

---

[1] The content in this subsection is written, based on the content in the paper [1] (Copyright(C)2022) published from IEICE.

© The Author(s), under exclusive license to Springer Nature Singapore Pte Ltd. 2025
I. Takanami, *Self-restructuring in Fault Tolerant Architecture*,
SpringerBriefs in Computer Science, https://doi.org/10.1007/978-981-96-1539-1_3

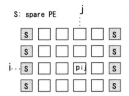

Fig. 3.1 Arrangement of OPSS schemes

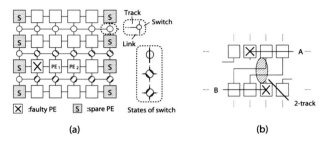

Fig. 3.2 a Interconnection structure for OP-STS. **b** c-paths A and B in near-miss relation need two tracks

For each faulty nonspare PE, there may be two straight c-paths which go on the left and right directions. Two opposite directional c-paths in the neighboring rows are called to be in "*near-miss*" relation if they overlap with two or more PEs (see Fig. 3.2b). A routing for c-paths in near-miss relation needs two tracks. Hence, for restructuring using single tracks, we have the following property.

Property 3.1 (Repairability condition) *Given an array of physical size $N \times (N + 2)$, it is restructurable into an array of logical size $N \times N$ if*

1. we can choose a continuous and straight c-path for each faulty nonspare PE, and
2. there is no "near-miss" among the c-paths chosen.   □

A restructuring algorithm satisfying Property 3.1 is given as follows.
      Restructuring algorithm (RA-OP-STS)

- Spares are on the left and right sides, i.e., PE[i, 0] and PE[i, $N + 1$] ($1 \le i \le N$).
- $A = (a_{ij})$ is a matrix with the same size as that of a fault pattern $P = (p_{ij})$.

Step 0: Setting.

Step 0-1. Set a_{ij} to 0 for all i and j ($1 \le i \le N, 0 \le j \le (N + 1)$)
Step 0-2. Set a_{i0} to p_{i0} for all i.
Step 0-3. Set sfg to 1.

Step 1: Increasing the variable j from 1 to N do

Step 1-1:   for all i $(1 \leq i \leq N)$ do
(i) Step 1-2:   if $p_{ij} = 0$ then set a_{ij} to $a_{i(j-1)}$
Step 1-3.   if $p_{ij} = 1$ then do
Step 1-4:   if $a_{i(j-1)} = 0$ then do
(ii) Step 1-5:   if $(a_{(i+1)(j-1)} \leq 1$ and $a_{(i-1)(j-1)} \leq 1)$, then set a_{ij} to 1 else do
(iii) Step 1-5-1:   if $p_{i(N+1)} = 0$ then set a_{ij} to 2
(iv) Step 1-5-2:   if $p_{i(N+1)} = 1$ then set sfg to 0 and goto Step 2.
(v) Step 1-6:   if $a_{i(j-1)} = 1$ and $p_{i(N+1)} = 0$ then set a_{ij} to 2;
(vi) Step 1-7:   if $a_{i(j-1)} = 1$ and $p_{i(N+1)} = 1$ then set sfg to 0, and goto Step 2.
(vii) Step 1-8:   if $a_{i(j-1)} = 2$ then set sfg to 0, and goto Step 2.

Step 2: if $sfg = 0$ then the fault pattern is unrepairable and goto Step 3 , else do

Step 2-1: if $p_{ij} = 1$ and $a_{ij} = 1$ then
P:E(i, j) is compensated for by the spare PE$(i, 0)$.
Step 2-2: if $p_{ij} = 1$ and $a_{ij} = 2$ then
PE(i, j) is compensated for by the spare PE$(i, N + 1)$.

Step 3: The algorithm ends.

The outline of the algorithm is as follows.
For all rows, inspecting the states of PEs from the leftmost column (0-th column) to the rightmost column ($(N + 1)$-th column), 0, 1, or 2 is marked to the respective PE. These marks are stored in the matrix A. The marks to the spare PEs on the 0-th column are the same as their fault states, i.e., 1's if they are faulty and 0's if heathy. A mark to a healthy PE is the same as that of its left neighbor while a mark to a faulty PE is different from that of its left neighbor. For a row (suppose it is i_0-th row), if a faulty PE(i_0, j') is met first, the situations of c-paths on the upper and lower neighbors are looked at and if there is no mark "2" implying a candidate c-path going from the left to the right of the j'-th column and if the spare at (i_0, j') is healthy, "1" is marked to PE(i_0, j'), which corresponds to Step 1-5. Then, PE(i_0, j') is compensated for by the spare on the left side (i.e., PE$(i_0, 0)$). Otherwise, the fault state of the spare on the right side (i.e., PE$(i_0, N + 1)$) is looked at with intension of compensating for the faulty PE(i_0, j') by it. If it is faulty, the value of $sfg = 0$ indicating irreparability is returned. If it is healthy, "2" is marked to the faulty PE(i_0, j') though at this time it can't yet be decided whether it can be compensated for by the spare on the right side.
If the above process is performed until $j = N$ and $sfg = 1$ is returned. The given fault pattern is repairable. Then, the faulty PEs marked "1" and "2" are compensated for by the spares at the left and the right sides, respectively.
The outline of the algorithm is stated formally as follows.

Theorem 3.1 (Repairability theorem) *An array of physical size $N \times (N + 2)$ with fault pattern $P = (p_{i,j})$ is restructured to an array of logical size $N \times N$ (in the meaning of Property 3.1) if and only if $sfg = 1$ is returned.*

Proof The statement is proved by a sequence of the following Properties and Lemmas. □

Property 3.2 *If PE(i, j) is healthy, $a_{ij} = a_{i(j-1)}$.*

Proof This is easily shown from the algorithm. □

Property 3.3 *We assume that the value sfg $= 1$ has been returned. Then, if $j' < j''$, $a_{ij'} \leq a_{ij''}$. In particular, PE(i, j'') is faulty if and only if $a_{i(j''-1)} < a_{ij''}$.*

Proof This is easily shown by the algorithm. □

Lemma 3.7 (Sufficient condition) *Let sfg $= 1$ at the end of the algorithm. Then for a faulty PE$(i, j)(N \geq j \geq 1)$, (1) if $a_{i(j-1)} < a_{ij} = 1$ it can be compensated for according to the c-path going to the left direction from PE(i, j), (2) if $a_{i(j-1)} < a_{ij} = 2$, it can be compensated for according to the c-path going to the right direction.*

Proof From the statement of Lemma, it is sufficient to consider how to take the c-path for a faulty PE(i, j) with $a_{i(j-1)} < a_{ij} = 1$ or $a_{i(j-1)} < a_{ij} = 2$. Hence, we will show that the conditions in Theorem 3.1 are satisfied if we take the c-path as above.

The proof of (1): From the hypothesis, $a_{i(j-1)} = 0$ and this implies that there is no faulty PE in the left direction of PE(i, j) from Property 3.3. Hence, there is no faulty PE on the path going to the left direction from PE(i, j). Next, in order to show that no near-miss occurs if such a path is taken as a c-path, it is sufficient to prove that for this path there does not exist such a faulty PE(i', j') that $a_{i'(j'-1)} < a_{i'j'} = 2$, $j' < j$, and $|i' - i| = 1$. If there exists such a faulty PE(i', j'), we would have $a_{ij} = 2$ from Step 1-5-1, which contradicts the hypothesis.

Proof of (2). Since $a_{ij} = 2$ and $a_{i(j-1)} = 0$ or 1, from Step 1-5-1 or (v) the spare PE$(i, N + 1)$ is healthy. Furthermore, there is no nonspare faulty PE at the right direction of PE(i, j) since if so, the algorithm will terminate by returning the value sfg $= 0$ from Step 1-8 against the hypothesis. Next, in order to show that no near-miss occurs, we must prove that there is no such a faulty PE(i', j') that $a_{i'(j'-1)} < a_{i'j'} = 1$, $j' > j$, and $|i' - i| = 1$ since if so, the path going to the right direction from PE(i, j) will overlap in more than one PE with the path going to the left direction from PE(i', j'). We suppose that there is such a faulty PE(i', j'). Then, since $a_{ij} = 2$ and $j' > j$, $a_{i(j'-1)} = 2$ from Property 3.3. Furthermore, since $|i' - i| = 1$ and $p_{i'j'} = 1$, $a_{i'j'} = 2$ from Step 1-5-1, which is a contradiction. □

Next, we will prove the necessary condition.

Property 3.4 *For a faulty PE(i, j), if $a_{ij} = 2$, then (1) for some j' $(0 \leq j' \leq j)$, PE(i, j') is faulty, or (2) for some (i', j') such that $|i' - i| = 1$ and $j' < j$, $a_{i'j'} = 2$ and PE(i', j') is faulty.*

Proof a_{ij} becomes 2 only if Step 1-5-1 or Step 1-6 is applied. When Step 1-5-1 is applied, there exists i' such that $|i' - i| = 1$, and $a_{i'(j-1)} = 2$. If PE$(i', j - 1)$ is healthy, $a_{i'(j-2)} = 2$ from Property 3.2. If PE$(i', j - 2)$ is healthy, $a_{i'(j-3)} = 2$, too. From the similar discussion, we can conclude that for some $j'(< j)$ PE(i', j') is faulty. This proves (2). When Step 1-6 is applied, $a_{i(j-1)} = 1$ and from Property 3.2 and the similar discussion above, we can show that (1) holds. □

Property 3.5 *Let $j_0 = min_{N \geq i \geq 1}\{j \mid PE(i, j)$ is faulty and $a_{ij}] = 2\}$ and let i for which j_0 is got be i_0. Then for some j' $(0 \leq j' \leq j_0)$, $PE(i - 1, j')$ is faulty.*

Proof This is easily shown from Property 3.4.   □

Property 3.6 *For a faulty $PE(i_0, j_0)$ with $a_{i_0 j_0} = 2$, if for all j' $(0 \leq j' \leq j_0)$ $PE(i_0, j')$ is healthy, the following holds.*

There exist a sequence (i_0, j_0), (i_1, j_1), $\cdots$, (i_k, j_k) such that $|i_p - i_{p-1}| = 1$, $p = 1, \cdots, k$ and $j_0 > j_1 > \cdots > j_k$, and $j_{k'}(< j_k)$ such that $PE(i_p, j_p)$ is faulty, $a_{i_p j_p} = 2$ $(p = 1, \cdots, k)$ and $PE(i_k, j_{k'})$ is faulty.

Proof This is easily shown from Properties 3.4 and 3.5.   □

Property 3.7 *A faulty $PE(i_0, j_0)$ with $a_{i_0 j_0} = 2$ cannot be compensated for by the spare at the left side, that is, it must be compensated for by the spare on the right side if possible. This means that we cannot take the c-path for it to the left direction.*

Proof For the case where the statement (1) in Property 3.4 is satisfied, this Property holds since there is a faulty PE on the left of $PE(i_0 j_0)$. For the case where the statement (2) in Property 3.4 is satisfied, there are such a sequence and faulty PEs as mentioned in Property 3.6. Then, since $PE(i_k, j_k)$ and $PE(i_k j_{k'})$ located at the left of $PE(i_k, j_k)$ are faulty, $PE(i_k, j_k)$ must be compensated for by the spare on the right side. Therefore, in order to avoid a near-miss, $PE(i_{k-1}, j_{k-1})$ must also be compensated for by the spare on the right side. From the similar discussion, $PE(i_0 j_0)$ must be compensated for by the spare on the right side.   □

Lemma 3.8 (Necessary condition) *If the value $sfg = 0$ is returned, the fault pattern is irreparable.*

Proof From Step 1-5-2, Step 1-7 and Step1-8, $sfg = 0$ only when for some (i, j) $(1 \leq i, j \leq N)$, $p_{ij} = 1$, and

(a) $a_{i(j-1)}] = 0$, for some i' and $|i' - i| = 1$ and $a_{i'(j-1)} = 2$, and $p_{i(N+1)} = 1$,
(b) $a_{i(j-1)}] = 1$ and $p_{i(N+1)} = 1$,

or

(c) $a_{i(j-1)}] = 2$.

Note that $PE(i, j)$ is faulty since $p_{ij} = 1$.

The case of (a). Since $a_{i'(j-1)} = 2$, for some $j_0(< j)$ $a_{i' j_0} = 2$ and $PE(i', j_0)$ is faulty. Therefore, from Property 3.7, $PE(i, j_0)$ must be compensated for by the spare $PE(i', N + 1)$. Then in order to avoid a near-miss, $PE(i, j)$ must also be compensated for by $PE(i', N + 1)$. However, since $p_{i(N+1)} = 1$, $PE(i, N + 1)$ is faulty. Hence, it is impossible to compensate for $PE(i, j)$.

The case of (b). Since $a_{i(j-1)} = 1$, there is a faulty PE to the left of $PE(i, j)$, and hence $PE(i, j)$ must be compensated for by the spare $PE(i, N + 1)$. However, this is impossible since $p_{i(N+1)} = 1$ and hence $PE(i, N + 1)$ is faulty.

The case of (c). There exists such a $j'(< j)$ that $a_{ij'} = 2$ and $PE(i, j')$ is faulty. From Property 3.7, $PE(i, j')$ must be compensated for by the spare on the right side. Therefore, the faulty $PE(i, j)$ must also be compensated for by the spare on the right side. However, this is impossible.   □

From the results above, Theorem 3.1 has been proved.

Figure 3.3 are examples of fault patterns with 12 faults judged to be repairable where the c-paths for the faulty PE(1,2), PE(2,2), PE(3,2), and PE(4,3) are leftward, and those for the faulty PE(1,3), PE(2,6), PE(3,8), PE(6,5), PE(7,2), and PE(8,6) are rightward. Note that the faulty spare PE(4,9) and PE(7,0) are compensated for by them-selves.

Similarly, Fig. 3.4 are examples of fault patterns with 12 faults judged to be unrepairable. It is seen that the faulty PE(3,8) has been judged to be unrepairable.

3.1.2   Hardware Realization of the Algorithm

We will describe a hardware realization of the algorithm RA-OP-STS. This repairs any fault pattern by self-restructuring if it satisfies the statement of Theorem 3.1, otherwise, outputs a signal indicating that it is unrepairable.

Figure 3.5 with 3.6 and 3.7 shows a circuit network to realize RA-OP-STS.

Figure 3.5 shows a circuit along a row Hence, there is practically such a circuit for each row and all the circuits operate in parallel. In the figure, the signals a_{ij} and

```
0 0 1 1 0 0 0 0 0 0
0 0 1 0 0 0 1 0 0 0
0 0 1 0 0 0 0 0 1 0
0 0 0 1 0 0 0 0 0 1
0 0 0 0 0 0 0 0 0 0
0 0 0 0 0 1 0 0 0 0
1 0 1 0 0 0 0 0 0 0
0 0 0 0 0 0 1 0 0 0
```

(a) a fault pattern P_1 with 12 faults.

```
0 0 1 2 2 2 2 2 2 0
0 0 1 1 1 1 2 2 2 0
0 0 1 1 1 1 1 1 2 0
0 0 0 1 1 1 1 1 1 0
0 0 0 0 0 0 0 0 0 0
0 0 0 0 0 2 2 2 2 0
1 1 2 2 2 2 2 2 2 0
0 0 0 0 0 0 2 2 2 0
```

(b) A matrix obtained in executing OP-STS for P_1

Fig. 3.3   A fault pattern P_1 judged to be repairable in RA-OP-STS

```
0 1 0 0 0 0 0 0 1 0
0 1 0 0 0 0 0 0 0 0
0 0 1 1 0 0 0 0 1 0
0 0 0 0 1 0 1 0 0 0
1 0 0 0 0 0 0 0 0 0
0 1 0 0 1 0 0 0 0 0
1 0 0 0 0 0 0 0 0 0
0 0 0 0 0 0 0 0 0 0
```

(a) a fault pattern P_2 with 12 faults,

```
0 1 1 1 1 1 1 1 2 0
0 1 1 1 1 1 1 1 1 0
0 0 1 2 2 2 2 2 3 0
0 0 0 0 2 2 3 3 0 0
1 1 1 1 1 1 0 0 0 0
0 1 1 1 2 2 0 0 0 0
1 1 1 1 1 1 0 0 0 0
0 0 0 0 0 0 0 0 0 0
```

(b) A matrix obtained in executing RA-OP-STS for P_2.

Fig. 3.4   A fault pattern P_2 judged to be unrepairable in RA-OP-STS

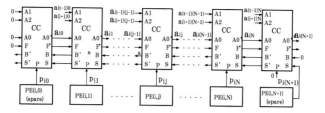

Fig. 3.5 CC-net

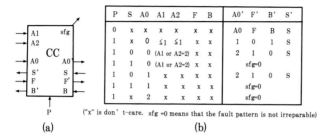

(a)   (b)

Fig. 3.6 The truth table of CC

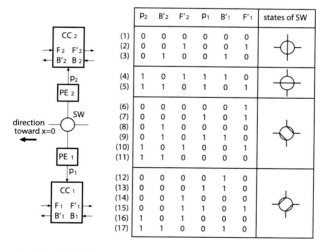

Fig. 3.7 The truth table of CC-SW

p_{ij} work in the same way as in the algorithm. Further, it is assumed that PE$[i, j]$ outputs the signal $p_{ij} = 1$ in some way when it is faulty. CC is the control circuit for switching connections of PEs whose truth table for defining the behavior is shown in Fig. 3.6b. Two signals each from two neighbors of the specified row are input to the terminals A_1 and A_2. Figure 3.7 shows the states of the switches set according to the signals of CC.

In what follows, we will prove that the behavior of the circuit is compatible with that of the algorithm RA-OP-STS. For convenience of explanation, CC to which p_{ij} is input is called CC of PE[i, j].

1. If $p_{i0} = 0$, 0 is input to the terminal P of CC of PE[$i, 0$] and hence from the truth table (b) in Fig. 3.6, a_{i0} = A0' = A0 = 0. Similarly, if $p_{i0} = 1$, a_{i0} = A0'= 1. Therefore, $a_{i0} = p_{i0}$, which corresponds to Step 0-2 in the algorithm.
2. The case where $p_{ij} = 0$. From the truth table, a_{ij} = A0' = A0 = $a_{i(j-1)}$, which corresponds to Step 1-2 in the algorithm.
3. The case where $p_{ij} = 1$ (that is, P = 1 of CC of PE(i, j)).

   (i) We assume $a_{i(j-1)}] = 0$. Then, A0 = 0. If all $a_{(i-1)(j-1)}$ = A1, $a_{(i+1)(i-1)}$ = A2 are less than or equal to 1, from the truth table $a_{ij}]$ = A0' = 1 which corresponds to Step 1-5. Otherwise, we suppose that any of A1 and A2 is 2. If $p_{i(N+1)} = 0$, S = 0 of every PE. Hence a_{ij} = A0' = 2 which corresponds to Step 1-5-1. If $p_{i(N+1)} = 1$, S = 1 of every PE. Hence f-$flag$ = 0 which corresponds to Step 1-5-2.

   (ii) We assume $a_{i(j-1)}] = 1$. Then, A0 = 1. If $p_{i(N+1)} = 0$, S = 0 and from the truth table $a_{ij}]$ = A0' = 2, which corresponds to Step 1-6. If $p_{i(N+1)} = 1$, S = 1 and f-$flag$ = 1 which corresponds to Step 1-8. □

From the discussion above, it has been proved that the behavior of the circuit is compatible with that of the algorithm.

Next, we describe that the states of switches are correctly set. As seen from Fig. 3.7, the switches are controlled by the signals F' and B', and the signals from the neighboring PEs. The truth table originally has 64 rows. However, only 17 rows are sufficient. First, from the truth table of CC in Fig. 3.6, "x11xxx", "xxxx11", "100xxx", and "xxx100" do not occur. The number of such six-tuples consisting of 0 or 1 is 39. Furthermore, the tuples "001010", "001110", "010001", "010101", "101010", and "110001" can't occur because if so, a near-miss will happen. Finally, for "101101" and "110110", the behaviors of switches are arbitrary, that is, *don't-care*. Excluding the above 47 tuples, the 17 tuples shown in Fig. 3.7 remain. Then we can ascertain that the behaviors of switches are correct by checking them for the 17 tuples.

The following figures are an illustration of hardware to realize the algorithm RA-OP-STS. Figure 3.8 is the contents of matrices *A* and *P* when the algorithm has been applied to the fault pattern in which squares marked with × are faulty PEs. The symbols like (i), ..., (vii) in A imply that the statements with the same symbols in the algorithm have been applied.

Figure 3.9 shows the signals around CCs.

Figure 3.10 shows the states of switches for connecting among PEs.

Fig. 3.8 An illustration of fault pattern and contents of matrices A and P after the algorithm has been executed

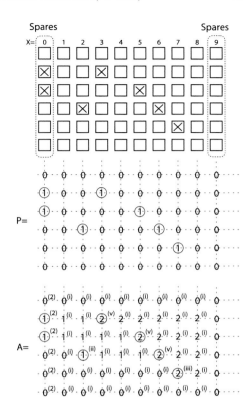

3.2 Spares on the Opposite Two Sides with Double-Track-Shift (OP-DTS)

Figure 3.11 is a interconnection structure with spares on the opposite two sides where only difference from STS scheme is that double tracks are used and hence, the near-miss relation is permissible. Then, the restructuring can be done independently for each row and realized easily by hardware.

3.2.1 Restructuring Algorithm (RA-OP-DTS)

Do the following steps.

Step 1: Set all the elements of $D = (d_{ij})$ to 0s and sfg to 1.

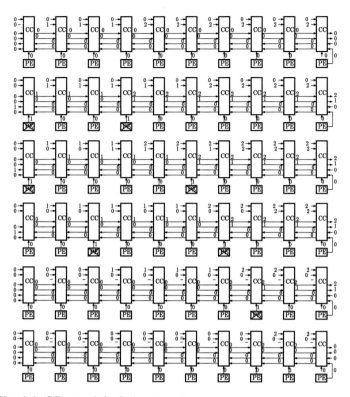

Fig. 3.9 Signals in CC network for fault pattern P

Step 2: Increasing the variable i from 1 to N, do Step 2.1 to 2.3.

Step 2-2: Set flg to p_{i0}.

Step 2-2: Increasing the value of j from 1 to N, do

Step 2-2-1: if ($p_{ij} = 1$ and $flg = 2$), then set sfg to 0 and goto Step 3.

Step 2-2-2: If ($p_{ij} = 1$ and $flg = 1$), then do

Step 2-2-2-1: set d_{ik} to 2,

Step 2-2-2-2: set flg to 2.

Step 2-3: If ($p_{ij} = 1$ and $flg = 0$), then do

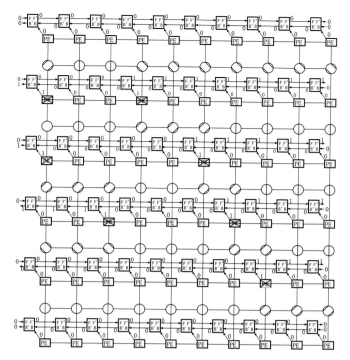

Fig. 3.10 States of switches on restructuring

Fig. 3.11 Double track shift method for OPSS

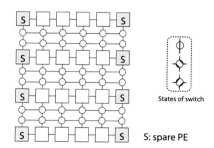

Step 2-3-1: set *flg* to 1,

Step 2-3-2: decreasing k from j to 1, do

Step 2-3-2-1: set d_{ik} to 1

Step 3: If $sfg = 0$, P is unrepairable. Otherwise, repairable.

Step 4: The algorithm ends.

The outline of RA-OP-DTS is as follows.

Scanning each row, it is checked what number of faulty PEs is. Then if it is one, the c-path is toward the left. If it is two, the c-path from the faulty PE located at the left (right) is toward the left (right). If it is more than two, the fault pattern is irreparable. Then, the following property is stated without the formal proof since the idea is simple.   □

Property 3.8 *A fault patter in OP-DTS is judged to be repairable if RA-OP-DTS returns the value of sfg = 1, otherwise unrepairable.*

3.2.2   Hardware Realization of the Algorithm

Figure 3.12 shows a hardware realization of RA-OP-DTS, where the function of CC is defined by the truth table Table 3.1 and the equations below.

Pairs (Q, R) corresponds to the value of *flg*, where $(0,0)$ to *flg* = 0, $(0,1)$ to 1 and (10) to 2. $(1,1)$ to *don't care*. $L = 1$ indicates $d = 1$ and a leftward c-path, $Q = 1$ indicates $d = 2$ and a rightward c-path.

$$R_o = \overline{p} \cdot R_i + p \cdot \overline{R_i} \ (= p \oplus R_i)$$
$$Q_o = Q_i + p \cdot R_i$$
$$L_o = L_i + p \cdot \overline{Q_i} \cdot R_i \ (= \overline{L_i + \overline{Q_i + R_i}})$$
$$sfg = \overline{p} + \overline{Q_i} \ (= \overline{p \cdot Q_i})$$

$$(3.1)$$

3.3   Spares on Orthogonal Sides with Direct Replacement (OT-DR)

Figure 3.13 shows the orthogonal side spare scheme in which spares PEs are located on the orthogonal sides of an array. Hence, $2N$ spares are located around an array

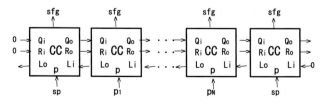

Fig. 3.12 op-DBL-CC

Table 3.1 Truth table of CC ($*$ means *don't care*)

p	Q_i	R_i	L_i	Q_o	R_o	L_o	sfg
1	0	0	0	0	1	1	1
1	0	0	1	0	1	1	1
1	0	1	0	1	0	0	1
1	0	1	1	1	0	1	1
1	1	0	0	$*$	$*$	$*$	0
1	1	0	1	$*$	$*$	$*$	0
1	1	1	0	$*$	$*$	$*$	0
1	1	1	1	$*$	$*$	$*$	0
0	a	b	c	a	b	c	1

Fig. 3.13 A PA with spares on the orthogonal sides

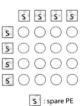

$\boxed{s}$: spare PE

with size of $N \times N$. For this scheme, the direct and STS replacing methods are treated with. First, the direct replacement (DR) method is described.[2]

In DR method, a faulty PE[i, j] at the i-th row and j-th column is directly replaced by either spare PE(0, j) in the 0-th row or spare PE(i, 0) in the 0-th column.

A strategy for deciding that by which spares faulty PEs should be replaced will be formalized as a matching problem in graph theory in Sect. 2.2. Now, a bipartite graph $G = (V, E)$ is constructed as follows. V is a set of vertices which consists of faulty PEs (including faulty spare PEs) and spare PEs which will replace the faulty PEs. E is a set of edges which consists of replacing relation where (p, s) in E means the faulty PE P will be replaced by the spare PE S. Then, G has a property that the degree of p (denoted as $deg(p)$), i.e., the number of edges incident to p, is less than or equal to 2. Using the property, a restructuring algorithm will be given in a convenient form for realizing it by hardware. The algorithm is given for a PA with an interconnection structure shown in Fig. 3.14, according to the property on the matching in graph theory.

Figure 3.15 illustrates the bipartite graph (compensation graph) for a PA with faulty PEs marked with $\times$'s, which consists of three connected components CC_1, CC_2 and CC_3.

The restructuring through replacement by spare is stated as follows, in terms of graph theory.

---

[2] The content in this subsection is written, based on the paper [2].

Fig. 3.14 Interconnection structure of a mesh array with switches for replacing faulty PEs where arrows indicate the directions to spares which replace faulty PEs

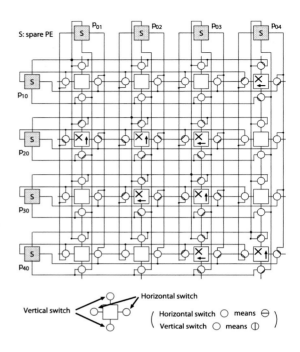

Property 3.9 *The set of faulty PEs V_f is repairable by replacement if and only if a matching from V_f to $(V_c \cup V_r)$ where V_c and V_r are the sets of spares in the 0-th row and column, respectively exists. For such a matching M, faulty p_{ij} is replaced by spare p_{i0} if $(p_{ij}, p_{i0}) \in M$, and by spare p_{0j} if $(p_{ij}, p_{0j}) \in M$.* ☐

Now, the restructuring algorithm will be given, using Theorem 2.2.

3.3.1 Restructuring Algorithm (RA-OT-DR)

- Notation: N_f denote the number of unrepaired faulty PEs in a row or column.

Input: An array with size of $N \times N$ with faulty PEs.

Step 1: Do the following (a) and (b) N times.

(a) Count the number of unrepaired faulty PEs (including a spare PE) toward a spare in each column. This is done in parallel for all columns. Then, replace a faulty PE in a column with $N_f = 1$ by a spare in the upper side and set N_f to 0.

(b) Count the number of unrepaired faulty PEs (including a spare PE) toward a spare in each row. This is done in parallel for all rows. Then, replace a faulty PE in a row with $N_f = 1$ by a spare on the left side and set N_f to 0.

Fig. 3.15 a An illustration of spare replacement with faulty PEs marked "×", and **b** its compensation graph which consists of three connected components CC_1, CC_2 and CC_3

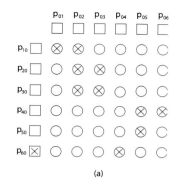

(a)

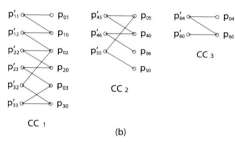

(b)

Step 2: If there is a column or row with $N_f \geq 3$, the array with faults is unrepairable, the signal indicating so is output and the repairing process is ended. Otherwise, go to the next step.

Step 3: If there is a column or row with $N_f = 2$ and the spare in the column or row is faulty, the array with faults is unrepairable, the signal indicating so is output and the repairing process is ended. Otherwise, go to the next step.

Step 4: The array is repairable and if $N_f = 0$ for all columns and rows, the repairing process is ended. Otherwise, go to the next step.

Step 5: A spare PE by which each unrepaired faulty PE in closed cycles will be replaced is determined as follows.

Beginning with the leftmost column, do the following.

(i) Check whether there are unrepaired faulty PEs in the column. This is done by sending a signal "1" from the lowest row in the column toward the upper. If it is confirmed that there is none, go to the column next to the right. Otherwise, there are unrepaired two faulty PEs in the column and one of them PE *A* located in the lower row than another PE *B* will receive the signal "1". Then, PE *A* sends signal "1"s to the left and right and is replaced by a spare PE located in the left side.

As a general rule,

(a) a faulty PE which has received a signal "1" from the upper or lower sends signal "1"s to the right and left, and is replaced by a spare PE located on the left side.

(b) a faulty PE which has received a signal "1" from the left or right sends signal "1"s to the upper and lower, and is replaced by a spare PE located in the upper side.

(c) A healthy or repaired PE only passes a signal which it has received.

(ii) Finally, a signal "1" must reach the PE A via PE B. If the column checked is the rightmost column, this process is ended. Otherwise, go to the column next to the right and go to (i).   □

Figure 3.16 shows an example of a repairable fault pattern where PE(3,1) is replaced by the spare PE(0, 1) in Step 1-(a) as shown in (b) and PE(1,5) is replaced by the spare PE(1, 0) in Step 1-(b) as shown in (c). The remaining faulty PEs are traced in a closed cycle as shown by the dotted line in (c). The cycle is traced, starting at PE(3, 2) received "1" signal from the bottom row. Then, the closed cycle consists of PE(3,2)→PE(3,5)→PE(5,5)→PE(5,4)→ PE(4,4)→PE(4,3)→PE(2,3)→ PE(2,2)→PE(3,2). (d) shows the signals "1s" at the faulty PEs and (e) shows the directions of the replacement.

Figures 3.17 and 3.18 are examples of unrepairable fault patterns where the former is judged in Step 3 and the latter in Step 2 as unrepairable, respectively.

3.3.2   Hardware Realization of the Algorithm

The above behavior of the restructuring algorithm is performed in hardware by logical circuits NET-1 and NET-2 to be described in the following.

Now, first, we show a logical circuit NET-1 which realizes from Steps 2 to 5 of RA-OT-DR. Next, we show a logical circuit NET-2 which decides the directions of replacements for faulty PEs in closed cycle in Step 6 of RA-OT-DR.

Logical circuit NET-1

Figure 3.19 shows NET-1 which consists of modules M_{PE}, M_{SP} and a gate G_1 where SP is a spare PE, M_{PE} is the module shown in (b), and M_{SP} is the module shown in (c) which contain submodules C_1s. We explain the functions of the modules.

The modules in NET-1;
Assumption:

- Each PE and SP outputs 1 as its fault signal if it is faulty, and 0 otherwise. The fault signal of a PE (SP) is input to the terminal F of M_{PE} (M_{SP}) as shown in Fig. 3.19.   □

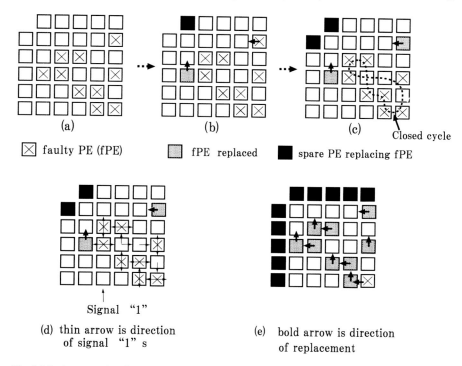

Fig. 3.16 An example of a repairable fault pattern

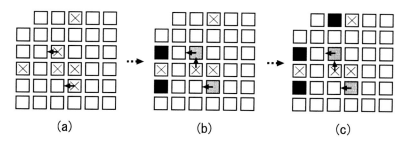

Fig. 3.17 An example of a fault pattern judged unrepairable in Step 3

Notation 3.6

- Input signal to a terminal n is denoted as i_n. The output signal out of a terminal m is denoted as o_m.
- $i(x, y)$ and $o(x, y)$ denote the input and output from M_{PE} in the x-th row and y-th column, respectively.
- $i(0, y)$ and $o(0, y)$ denote the input and output from M_{SP} in the y-th column, that is, upper side, respectively.

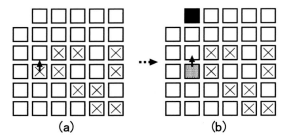

(a)   (b)

Fig. 3.18 An example of an unrepairable fault pattern judged in Step 2

Table 3.2 Behavior of G_2 and G_3

i_5^t	i_8^t	o_U^t	o_L^t
0	0	$o_U^{(t-1)}$	$o_L^{(t-1)}$
0	1	1	0
1	0	0	1
1	1	0	0

- $i(x, 0)$ and $o(x, 0)$ denote the input and output from M_{SP} in the x-th row, that is, left side, respectively.
- $N_f(0, y)$ ($N_f(x, 0)$) denotes the number of unrepaired faulty PEs in the y-th column (x-th row).   □

- The function of C_1

    C_1 is used to count N_f in a row or a column and check whether $N_f > 2$. To do so, C_1 adds binary numbers $(x_1 x_0)_2$ and $(0f)_2$, and outputs a binary number $(y_1 y_0)_2$ but the sum is fixed to 3, that is, $(11)_2$ if it is greater than 2.

- The function of M_{PE}

1. If both the signals i_5 and i_8 of the terminals 5 and 8 are 1s (so initially as will be shown in 1 of the behavior of NET-1), $o_f = i_F$, and 0 otherwise.
2. If $i_F = 1$ (so if the PE is faulty), the outputs o_U^t and o_L^t of the gate G_2 and G_3 at time t are as shown in Table 3.2, according to the signals i_5^t and i_8^t of the terminals 5 and 8 at time t. This means that the combination of G_2 and G_3 works as a flip-flop with the inputs i_5 and i_8.

- The function of M_{SP}

1. If $o_5 = 1$, that is, the output of FF is 1, the output $y_1 y_0$ of C_1 becomes as shown in Table 3.3.
2. When a clock is input to FF through CK-U (CK-L), if $N_f \leq 1$ in a column (row), Q of FF becomes 0, i.e., $o_5 = 0$. Otherwise 1, i.e., $o_5 = 1$.

Table 3.3 Behavior of C_1

$(x_1\,x_0)_2 + (0\,i_F)_2$	$y_1\,y_0$
$(0\,0)_2$	0 0
$(0\,1)_2$	0 1
$(1\,0)_2$	1 0
$\geq (1\,1)_2$	1 1

The behavior of NET-1

1. The behavior of NET-1 is controlled by the clocks input to the terminals CK-U and CK-L which are alternatively N times given for an array with size of $N \times N$ as $ck\text{-}u(1)$, $ck\text{-}\ell(1)$, ... , $ck\text{-}u(N)$, $ck\text{-}\ell(N)$ where $ck\text{-}u(i)$ and $ck\text{-}\ell(i)$ are the i-th clocks to CK-U and CK-L, respectively.

2. Initially, the flip-flop FF in each M_{SP} is set to 1, that is, o_5 of each M_{SP} is 1. Then, i_5 and i_8 of each M_{PE} are 1s, and the output of C_1 in each M_{SP} $(y_1\,y_0)_2$ shows N_f in the row or column.

3. When a clock through CK-U is input to FF of M_{SP},
   (i) if $N_f(0, y) \leq 1$, $o_5(0, y)$ becomes 0 and $o_1(0, y) = i_2(0, y)$. Moreover,
   · If $N_f(0, y) = 0$ or $(N_f(0, y) = 1$ and the spare PE$(0, y)$ is faulty), o_U, o_L and o_f of each M_{PE} in the y-th column become 0's, respectively.
   · If $N_f(0, y) = 1$ and the spare PE$(0, y)$ is not faulty (this means there exists a single unrepaired faulty PE(x, y) for some x), $o_U(x, y)$ and $o_f(x, y)$ become 1 and 0, respectively (this mean PE(x, y) is replaced by the spare PE$(0, y)$ and $N_f(0, y)$ becomes 0, which corresponds to Step 2 in RA-OT-DR, and o_U's and o_L's of all the other M_{PE}'s in the y-th column become 0's because i_F of $M_{PE}(x, y)$ is 1, those of the other M_{PES} in the y-th column are 0's, $i_5 = 0$ and $i_8 = 1$). Note that if $N_f(0, y) = 1$ just before $ck\text{-}u(i)$ is input, there exists a single unrepaired PE(x, y), and $N_f(0, y) \geq 2$ and $N_f(x, 0) \geq 2$ when $ck\text{-}u(j)$ and $ck\text{-}\ell(j)$ are input for any $j < i$.
   (ii) if $N_f(0, y) \geq 2$, $o_5(0, y) = 1$.

4. When a clock through CK-L is input, the similar move to that in above 3 is performed where "column" is replaced by "row". Note that if $N_f(x, 0) = 1$ just before $ck\text{-}\ell(i)$ is input, there exists a single unrepaired PE(x, y), and $N_f(x, 0) \geq 2$ and $N_f(0, y) \geq 2$ when $ck\text{-}\ell(j)$ and $ck\text{-}ul(j)$ are input for any $j < i$.

5. The clocks through CK-U and CK-L are alternatively N times given. A faulty PE whose o_f is 0 has been repaired. After this, such a faulty PE is not counted in N_f because o_f is 0. This corresponds to Step 2 in RA-OT-DR.

6. $o_{UNREC} = 1$ if and only if o_1 of some M_{SP} is 1 if and only if $N_f > 2$ or ($N_f = 2$ including a faulty spare) in a row or a column. Hence, $o_1 = 1$ of some M_{SP} corresponds to Steps 4 or 5 in RA-OT-DR and $o_{UNREC} = 1$ of NET-1 indicates that the array with the faults is unrepairable (Fig. 3.19).

7. If $o_{UNREC} = 0$, o_1's of all M_{SP}'s are 0's, which indicates that the array with the faults is repairable. Then, if there is neither row nor column such that $N_f = 2$, the spare is healthy and o_5 of M_{SP} is 1, this repairing process can be successfully

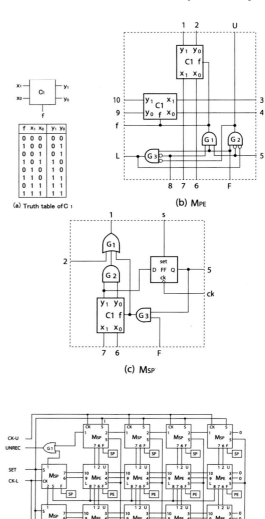

Fig. 3.19 NET-1 for executing Steps 1 to 4 in RA-OT-DR

ended. However, for simplicity, omitting this check, we go to the process for finding closed cycles (even if there may not be such cycles) of Step 6 in RA-OT-

DR together with the directions of replacing for faulty PEs in the cycles. The process is realized by the network NET-2 shown in Fig. 3.20.

Logical circuit NET-2

- The function of the module M+

1. The terminal f of M_{PE} in NET-1 is connected to the terminal F of M+.
2. If i_F $(= o_f)$ is 0, the internal structure becomes as shown in Fig. 3.20b, i.e., the signals pass through horizontally and vertically.
3. If i_F is 1, the internal structure becomes as shown in Fig. 3.20a.
   The signal through x_3 from the top or x_1 from the bottom are transferred to the left through y_4 and the right through y_2, and the signal is stored in the flip-flop FF$_L$ which indicates that the direction of replacement is to the left.
   the signal through x_4 from the left or x_2 from the right are transferred to the lower through y_1 and the upper through y_3, and the signal is stored in the flip-flop FF$_U$ which indicates that the direction of replacement is to the upper.

The behavior of NET-2

Note that (i) The internal structure of M_+ becomes as shown in Fig. 3.20b if a PE with the M_+ is healthy or has been repaired and in (a) if it has not yet been repaired, and (ii) There are exactly two unrepaired faulty PEs in a row or column in a closed cycle.

1. Initially, all the flip-flops are reset.
2. Signal 1 is shifted from the left to the right in the shift-register at the time when a clock pulse is given to CLK-1.
3. For $i = 1$ to N, the following is performed.
   (i) A clock is fed to CLK-2. Q_i of the shift-register becomes 1. This signal "1" is input to x_1 of M_+ in the bottom row of i-th column. At the time, the output of the gate G_1 becomes 1 and hence a clock to CLK-1 is inhibited to be supplied to the shift register. While a clock to CLK-1 is not supplied, the signal "1" input to the i-th column behaves as follows.

   - If there is no unrepaired faulty PE in the i-th column, the signal "1" passes through all the M_+s in the column, turns back at the M_+ in the top row of the column (note that the terminals x_5 and y_3 are connected) and reaches the terminal y_5 of the M_+ in the bottom row of the column.
   - If there are unrepaired faulty PEs, there are exactly two such PEs in the column which are denoted as M_+^L and M_+^U where the former is in a lower location. The signal "1" is fed to M_+^L and propagates in a closed cycle as mentioned in Step 5 in RA-OT-DR, finally reaches M_+^U, sent in the upper direction, turn back at M_+ in the top row and reaches the terminal y_5 of the M_+ in the bottom row of the column.

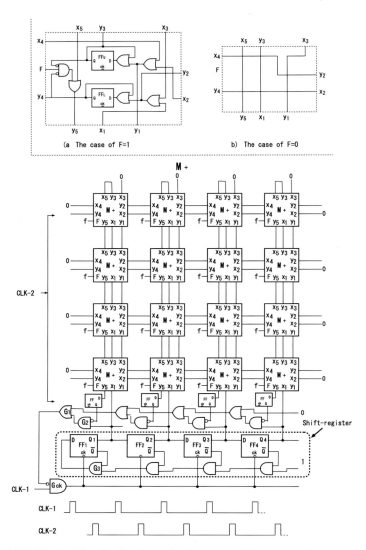

Fig. 3.20 NET-2 for deciding the directions of replacement while executing Step 5 in RA-OT-DR

- The signal "1" which reaches y_5 of the M_+ in the bottom row as above is
  memorized in the D-FF by a clock to CLK-2 and fed to the gate G_2. Then,
  the outputs of G_2 and G_1 become 0s, and hence, a clock to CLK-1 can pass
  through the gate G_{ck}.

As explained so far, Net-1 and -2 exactly performs each step of RA-OT-DR.

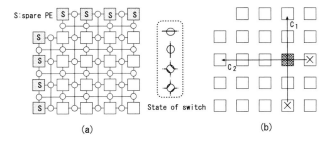

Fig. 3.21 **a** OTSS using single track switches. **b** c-paths c_1 and c_2 in intersection relation

3.4 Spares on Orthogonal Sides with STS Replacement (OT-STS)

Spares are arranged as in Figs. 3.13 and 3.21 shows an interconnection structure with c-paths in interconnection relation . This is a mesh-connected PA proposed by Kung et al. [3] except that it has only one spare row and one spare column. Tracks consisting of links and switches run along toward the spares located on the upper and left sides. A single track runs between adjacent rows and columns, and there is a switch at the cross of a track and a link connecting PEs.[3]

3.4.1 Restructuring Algorithm (RA-OT-STS)

The replacement of a faulty PE is done as follows. A faulty PE marked with $\times$ is bypassed in the horizontal and vertical directions and replaced by its adjacent healthy PE in either horizontal or vertical direction, which in turn is replaced by the next adjacent healthy PE, and so on. This replacement is repeated until a healthy spare PE is used in the end. This process defines a compensation path (c-path), which is a set of straight and continuous PEs from a faulty PE to a healthy spare PE. Then, we have the following property.

Property 3.10 (Repairability condition for RA-OT-STS) *An array with faulty PEs is repairable if and only if there is a set of c-paths S such that*

1. *S contains a c-path for each nonspare faulty PE, and*
2. *No c-paths in S are in intersection relation.* □

Note that the condition is not necessary but sufficient.

We present a restructuring algorithm (RA-OT-STS) by which we can judge whether the condition of Property 3.10 is satisfied for an array with faulty PEs whose physical size is $(N + 1) \times N + 1)$ while it's logical size is $N \times N$.

---

[3] The content in this subsection is written, based on the content in the paper [4] (Copyright(C)2022) published from IEICE.

We will give an restructuring algorithm satisfying the condition of Property 3.10.

Notation 3.7

- p_{ij} is the faulty state of PE(i, j).
- Spares are on the upper and left sides, i.w., they are at $(0, j)$'s $(1 \leq j \leq N)$ and at $(i, 0)$'s $(1 \leq i \leq N)$.
- A matrix $P = (p_{ij})$ is a fault pattern.
- $D = (d_{ij})$ be a matrix with the same size as that of P.
- *sfg* and *flg* are flags.

[RA-OT-STS]

Step 0: Setting.
(1) Step 0-1: Set d_{ij} to 0 for all i, j $(0 \leq i \leq N)$, $(0 \leq j \leq N)$.
(2) Step 0-2: Set *sfg* to 1.
      Step 1: Decreasing j from N to 1 do
(3)   Step 1-1: Set *flg* to p_{0j};
      Step 1-2: Increasing i from 1 to N do
(4)   Step 1-2-1: If $d_{ij} = 2$ then set *flg* to 1;
         Step 1-2-2: If ($p_{ij} = 1$ and *flg* $= 1$) then do
(5)   Step 1-2-2-1: set d_{ij} to 2;
            Step 1-2-2-2: Decreasing k from $j - 1$ to 0 do
(6)   Step 1-2-2-2-1: if $p_{ik} = 1$ then set *sfg* to 0 and goto Step 2
(7)   Step 1-2-2-2-2: else set d_{ik} to 2
      Step 1-3: if ($p_{ij} = 1$ and *flg* $= 0$) then do
(8)   Step 1-3-1: Set *flg* to 1;
         Step 1-3-2: Decreasing k from i to 0 do
(9)   Step 1-3-2-1: Set d_{kj} to 1;
Step 2: If *sfg* $= 0$, P is unrepairable. Otherwise, repairable.
Step 3: End.   □

From the algorithm, we can see the following. If $p_{ij} = 1$ and *flg* $= 1$, a sequence of $d_{ik} = 2$'s $(k \leq j)$ is generated in the left direction from PE(i, j) toward the spare on the left side in the processes (5) and (7) in the algorithm. This sequence which reaches the spare is called 2-sequence from PE(i, j) which is denoted as 2-seq(i, j). Similarly, if $p_{ij} = 1$ and *flg*$= 0$, a sequence of $d_{kj} = 1$'s is generated in the upper direction from PE(i, j) toward the spare on the upper side in the process (9). This sequence is called 1-sequence from PE(i, j) which is denoted as 1-seq(i, j). 1- and 2-sequences are candidate c-paths.

Figure 3.22 shows illustrations of 1- and 2 sequences generated for repairable and unrepairable fault patterns where the superscript i of $1^{(i)}$ or $2^{(i)}$ denotes the label of the process executed in the algorithm.

The process executing RA-OT-STS is outlined as follows.

1. Starting at the rightmost column, that is, N-th column, we try to find an upward c-path from a selected faulty PE to a spare on the upper side where PEs are

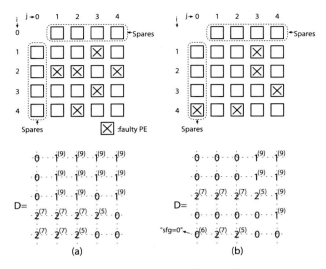

Fig. 3.22 **a** A repairable fault pattern and the content of matrix D. **b** An unrepairable fault pattern and the content of matrix D after the algorithm has been applied

sequentially selected from the top row to the bottom row. In this case, a sequence of 1's from the selected PE is generated.

2. Otherwise, we try to find a leftward c-path toward a spare on the left side. In this case, a sequence of 2's from the selected PE is generated.

3. If the above processes are successful for all PEs in the column, that is, $sfg = 1$, the similar processes are executed on the column next to the left, and so on.

4. If the above processes are at last successfully executed on the left-most column, the algorithm ends by returning $sfg = 1$ and the fault pattern is judged to be repairable. Then, a faulty PE[i, j] is repaired by upward (leftward) shifting according to 1-seq(i, j) (2-seq(i, j)).

5. Otherwise, the algorithm ends by returning $sfg = 0$ and the fault pattern is judged to be unrepairable.

Then we have the following property for repairability.

Property 3.11 *An array of physical size $(N + 1) \times (N + 1) - 1$ with a fault pattern $P = (p_{ij})$ can be restructured into an array of logical size $N \times N$ (in the meaning of Property 3.10) if and only if RA-OT-STS ends by returning $sfg = 1$. If it ends by returning $sfg = 1$, the set of 1- and 2-sequences is a set of c-paths which satisfies the RC of Property 3.10.*

Proof See [4].   □

3.4.2 Hardware Realization of RA-OT-STS

We will describe a hardware realization of RA-OT-STS. It repairs any fault pattern by self-restructuring if it satisfies the repairability condition, and otherwise, outputs a signal indicating that it is unrepairable.

Figure 3.23 shows a network performing RA-OT-STS. Each PE has a logical circuit CC shown in Fig. 3.23a, which is connected as shown in Fig. 3.23b. CC has four input signals p, D_{in}, L_{in} and U_{in} and four output signals D_{out}, L_{out}, U_{out} and S_{fg}. Table 3.4 is the truth table for these signals. p corresponds to p_{ij} in RA-OT-STS, D_{in} and D_{out} at (i, j) to the flg_{ij} and flg'_{ij}, where the former and the latter are the values of flg just before and after for-process at (i, j) is executed, respectively (see Notation 2.5). L_{in} and L_{out} to input and output of 2-sequence, respectively, U_{in} and U_{out} to input and output of 1-sequence, respectively and S_{fg} to s_{fg}. Describing more detail, the correspondence between the behaviors of CC and RA-OT-STS is as follows.

1. That D_{out}'s in rows from (1) to (8) in Table 3.4 are 1's corresponds to that in RA-OT-STS if $p_{ij} = 1$, flg becomes 1.
2. That D_{out}'s in rows (11), (12), (15), and 16) are 1's corresponds to (4) in RA-OT-STS.
3. That D_{out}'s in rows (13) and (14) are 1's and That D_{out}'s in rows (9) and (10) are 0's are due to that none of from (4) to (10) in RA-OT-STS are applied and flg does not change.
4. The first row in Table 3.4 corresponds to (9) and (10) in RA-OT-STS and causes the origin of 1-sequence.
5. The rows (3) and (7) correspond to (6) in the algorithm and hence, $S_{fg} = 0$.
6. The row (5) corresponds to (5) in the algorithm and causes the origin of 2-sequence.
7. The row (9) corresponds to the case where a healthy PE is not on a c-path.
8. The row (10) corresponds to the case where 1-sequence passes a healthy PE.
9. The row (11) corresponds to the case where 2-sequence passes a healthy PE.
10. The row (12) corresponds to the case where 1- and 2-sequences intersect each other. However, since it could be proved that if $D_{out}(x, y) = 1$, $U_{in}(x, y) = 0$, this case never occurs in the steady state.
11. The row (13) corresponds to the case where PE is healthy, and none of from (4) to (10) in RA-OT-STS are applied.
12. The row (15) corresponds to the case where 2-sequence passes a healthy PE.

In the following, we will describe without the formal prove that the behavior of CC is compatible with that of RA-OT-STS, referring to Table 3.4. (The formal proof is long and tedious (see [4])). For convenience of explanation, the terminal names and the signals from/in the terminals are often identically used unless confused, and the signals from/in CC of PE(x, y) are denoted with index '(x, y)'.

From Table 3.4, we have the following logical equations.

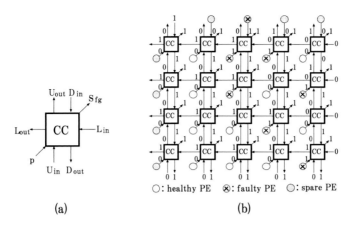

Fig. 3.23 A network performing RA-OT-STS in hardware. **a** Input and output signals of control circuit CCs. **b** Connection of CC and an illustration of inputs and outputs to/from CCs for a fault pattern

Table 3.4 Truth table ($*$ means *don't care*)

	p	D_{in}	L_{in}	U_{in}	D_{out}	L_{out}	U_{out}	S_{fg}
(1)	1	0	0	0	1	0	1	1
(2)	1	0	0	1	1	$*$	$*$	$*$
(3)	1	0	1	0	1	$*$	$*$	0
(4)	1	0	1	1	1	$*$	$*$	$*$
(5)	1	1	0	0	1	1	0	1
(6)	1	1	0	1	1	$*$	$*$	$*$
(7)	1	1	1	0	1	$*$	$*$	0
(8)	1	1	1	1	1	$*$	$*$	$*$
(9)	0	0	0	0	0	0	0	1
(10)	0	0	0	1	0	0	1	1
(11)	0	0	1	0	1	1	0	1
(12)	0	0	1	1	1	$*$	$*$	$*$
(13)	0	1	0	0	1	0	0	1
(14)	0	1	0	1	1	$*$	$*$	$*$
(15)	0	1	1	0	1	1	0	1
(16)	0	1	1	1	1	$*$	$*$	$*$

$$D_{out} = p + D_{in} + L_{in} \tag{3.2}$$

$$L_{out} = L_{in} + p \cdot D_{in} \tag{3.3}$$

$$U_{out} = U_{in} + p \cdot \overline{D}_{in} \tag{3.4}$$

$$\overline{S}_{fg} = p \cdot L_{in} \tag{3.5}$$

As shown in Fig. 3.23b, signals loop up and down. However, as shown in Lemma 2.1, the signals become stable for any fixed inputs.

In the following, we assume that the signals have become stable.

Property 3.12 *An array with faulty PEs is repairable, i.e., the repairability condition for OT-STS (Property 3.10) is satisfied if and only if all the output signals S_{fg}'s from CC's are 1's.*   ☐

Now, we discuss how to switch the connections among PEs if AND of all the output signals S_{fg}'s from CC's is 1. Hence, in the following, we assume that a repairable fault pattern is given. In order to switch the connections among PEs correctly, it is necessary and sufficient to know the correspondence between 1- or 2-sequences and the signals in the circuit.

Property 3.13 $d_{xy} = 2$ *if and only if $L_{out}(x, y) = 1$.*

☐

Property 3.14 $d_{xy} = 1$ *if and only if $U_{out}(x, y) = 1$.*   ☐

From the results above, it has been shown that there are one-to-one correspondences between 1-sequences and sequences of U_{out}'s, and between 2-sequences and sequences of L_{out}'s. Using this result, we could give a truth table defining the states of switches like Table 3.1. However, since it is a simple task, it will be omitted.

3.4.3 Algorithm for Spares on Rotated Sides (ROT-OT-STS)

The orthogonal spare side rotation method (shortly written as ROT method) to be proposed uses RA-OT-STS as a basic algorithm. While in RA-OT-STS spares are fixed on the left and upper sides of an array, in ROT method they are flexibly assigned on one of the four orthogonal sides which are the left and upper, the upper and right, the right and lower, and the lower and left sides. These assignments are denoted as Rot-0, Rot-90, Rot-180, and Rot-270, respectively as shown in Fig. 3.24.[4]

ROT method is done as follows.

RA-OT-STS is applied to each of the modified fault patterns according to the four assignments which are defined as in Eq. 3.6 where RA-OT-STS is performed with $G = (g_{ij})$ obtained by the coordinate transformation as below for x and y of an original fault pattern $P = (p_{xy})$.

The coordinate transformation is given by

$$\begin{pmatrix} i \\ j \end{pmatrix} = \begin{pmatrix} b_1 \\ b_2 \end{pmatrix} + \begin{pmatrix} a_{11} & a_{12} \\ a_{21} & a_{22} \end{pmatrix} \begin{pmatrix} x \\ y \end{pmatrix} \tag{3.6}$$

The parameters $b_1, b_2, a_{11}, ..., a_{22}$ are determined for each of Rot-0, -90, -180, and -270 as in Table 3.5.

---

[4] The content in this subsection is written, in part based on the paper [5].

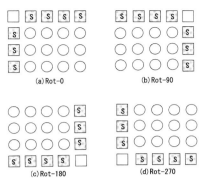

Fig. 3.24 Four assignments of spares on orthogonal sides

Table 3.5 The parameters b_1, b_2, a_{11}, ..., a_{22} for the respective rotations

	b_1	b_2	a_{11}	a_{12}	a_{21}	a_{22}
Rot-0	0	0	1	0	0	1
Rot-90	N	0	0	−1	1	0
Rot-180	N	N	−1	0	0	−1
Rot-270	0	N	0	1	−1	0

For example, the matrix $G = (g_{ij})$ transformed from $P = (p_{xy})$ by Rot-90 is as below and denoted as G_{rot-90}.

$$P = \begin{bmatrix} p_{00} & p_{01} & \cdots & p_{0N} \\ p_{10} & p_{11} & \cdots & p_{1N} \\ & \cdots\cdots\cdots \\ p_{N0} & p_{N1} & \cdots & p_{NN} \end{bmatrix}$$

$$G_{rot-90} = \begin{bmatrix} p_{0N} & p_{1N} & \cdots & p_{NN} \\ & \cdots\cdots\cdots \\ p_{01} & p_{11} & \cdots & p_{N1} \\ p_{00} & p_{10} & \cdots & p_{N0} \end{bmatrix}$$

Then, each of the modified RA-OT-STSs is applied at a time to an array with faults and if at least one of them ends with $sfg = 1$, the array with faulty PEs is judged to be repairable and the array is called to be **ROT-repairable**.

Instead of the above, one to fix the spares on one of the four orthogonal sides is called **nonROT** method.

Figure 3.25 shows a fault pattern which is repairable for Rot-180 but not the other Rot-*'s. That is, though the pattern is not repairable for the statically fixed spare

Fig. 3.25 A fault pattern which is repairable in Rot-180 but not the other Rot-∗'s

assignments as in Rot-0, Rot-90, and Rot-270, it is ROT-repairable. This suggests that ROT method may increase array reliabilities.

3.4.4   Hardware Realization of ROT-OT-STS

To realize ROT method in hardware, it is sufficient to rotate the CCs in Fig. 3.23 for the respective rotation degrees, i.e., 90°, 180° and 270°, and properly give the signal 0s to the CCs on the sides of the CC network. Figures 3.26 and 3.27 show how to rotate them by adding sw's and lines around the CC and changing the switch states of the sw's as shown, according to the respective degrees. This CC modified is denoted as ex-CC and the CC network composed of ex-CCs is denoted as ex-CC network. Figure 3.28 shows how to give the signal 0s to the sides of ex-CC network for each rotation.

3.4.5   Array Reliabilities

Figures 3.29 and 3.30 show the reliabilities of arrays with sizes of 8×8 and 16×16, respectively,

It is seen that the ARs for ROT method (denoted as Rot-full) fairly increase, comparing with those for nonROT method (nonRot-0) and OTSTS-cent+1 and -+2, where OTSTS-cent+1 and -+2 are shown for comparison. Here, OTSTS-cent+1 and -+2 are the ARs for the variants of OTSTS in terms of spare placement as shown in Fig. 3.31. OTSTS-cent+1 is the result when RA-OT-STS is applied once in order of 1st, 2nd, 3rd, and 4th quadrants. OTSTS-cent+2 is the result when RA-OT-STS is applied four times where it is applied the first time in order of 1st, 2nd, 3rd, and 4th quadrants, the second time in order of 2nd, 3rd, 4th, and 1st quadrants, the third time in order of 3rd, 4th, 1st, and 2nd quadrants, and the fourth time in order of 4th, 1st, 2nd, and 3rd quadrants. All the results are obtained by Monte Carlo simulation.

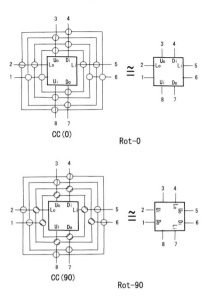

Fig. 3.26 States of sw's to rotate CC in CC network for the degrees 0° and 90°. CCs rotated are denoted as ex-CC(0) and ex-CC(90), respectively

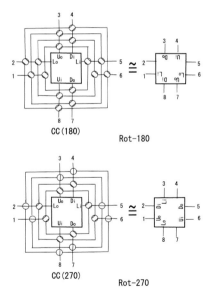

Fig. 3.27 States of sw's to rotate CC in CC network for the degrees 180° and 270°. CCs rotated are denoted as ex-CC(180) and ex-CC(270), respectively

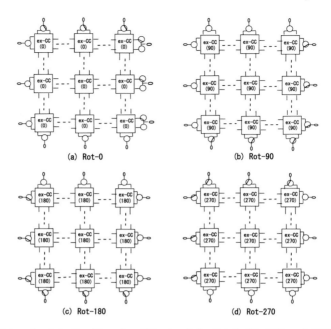

Fig. 3.28   States of sw's on the sides of ex-CC network for Rot-0, -90, -180, and -270, respectively

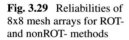

Fig. 3.29   Reliabilities of 8x8 mesh arrays for ROT- and nonROT- methods

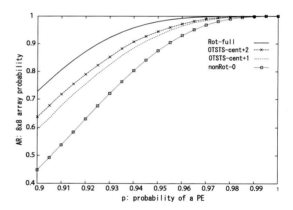

3.5   Degradable Restructuring by Direct Replacement

In the degradation approach, all PEs are considered in a uniform manner in the absence of spare PEs to construct a subarray, avoiding faulty PEs but keeping the mesh structure so that it's size is as large as possible. Then degradable 2D arrays linked with four-port switches have been extensively studied. Kuo and Chen studied the degradable reconfiguration problem under the certain routing constraints and showed that most reconfiguration problems under the rerouting constraints are

Fig. 3.30 Reliabilities of 16x16 mesh arrays for ROT- and nonROT- method

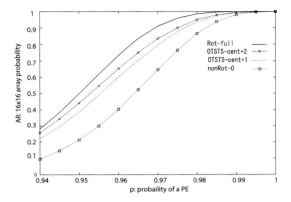

Fig. 3.31 A variant in terms of spare replacement where the row and column of spares are placed in the center of an array

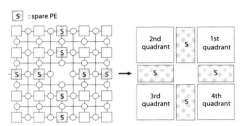

NP-complete [6]. Low et al. proposed an optimal algorithm, termed GCR to construct a maximum logical array (MLA) containing the selected rows [7]. Fukushi et al. used genetic approaches to evolve rerouting strategies for constructing logical rows/columns in designing the MLA [8, 9].

In the redundancy approach mentioned until now, a mesh-connected PA replaces faulty PEs by spare PEs so that the original logical size of the array is preserved. However, if all faulty PEs in an array are not replaced by spares due to the insufficient number of spares and/or the restructuring ability, the array is considered to be faulty and never used. As far as we know, the degradation and redundancy approaches are studied separately. So, it is hoped that a PA with faulty PEs which is not repairable is reused by reducing their sizes.

Here, we present a restructuring method with the degradation, and built-in circuits to realize the method. The method will make a system be reused more.

Now, it was described in the former section that how to replace faulty PEs with which spares is formalized as a matching problem in graph theory. Then, if no matching, i.e. no spare assignment, is found for an array with faulty PEs, rows and/or columns are deleted from the array so that a matching is successfully found for a degraded array. Finally, a hardware to realize the above process is presented. This leads to the realization of a degradable self-restructuring of processor arrays.[5]

---

[5] The content in this subsection is written, in part based on the paper [10].

3.5.1 Degradable Restructuring Algorithm (DRA-OT-DR)

Now, the degradation of an array is done by deleting functionally (or logically) rows and/or columns of an array. Then, the degradation changes the compensation graph as follows.

Suppose that the i-th row r_i (the i-th column c_i) corresponding to p_{i0} (p_{0i}) in the compensation graph is functionally deleted. Then, p_{i0} (p_{0i}) and faulty vertices p's such that (p', p_{i0})s $((p', p_{0i})$s) are deleted, including the edges incident to p's. Such a deletion of a row (column) may reduce the degrees of some vertices in V_2, which is called **D-deletion** in the following. With the situation in mind, a degradable restructuring algorithm with direct replacement (shortly written as **DRA-OT-DR**) is given as follows.

DRA-OT-DR

Step 1: Let $M = \phi$ (empty set), $E' = E$, $V_1' = V_1$ and $V_2' = V_2$.
Step 2: While there is a vertex v with $deg(v) = 1$ in V_2', do the following.
For $(w, v) \in E'$, let $M = M \cup \{(w, v)\}$, $\hat{E} = \{(w, \hat{v})|(w, \hat{v})$ in E'$\}$, $E' = E' - \hat{E}$, $V_1' = V_1' - \{w\}$ and $V_2' = V_2' - \{v\}$.
Step 3: If $V_1' = \phi$, M is a matching from V_1 to V_2 and go to Step 6.
Step 4: If there is a vertex v in V_2' whose degree is more than 2, select and D-delete vertices in V_2' so that the degree of v becomes less than or equal to 2. Further, if there is a vertex u in V_1' whose degree is 1, D-delete w where (u, w) in E and go to Step 2, otherwise go to Step 5.
Note that the degree of any faulty nonspare vertex except faulty spare vertex is two and that of any faulty spare vertex is one.
Step 5: Let $\hat{G} = (\hat{V}_1, \hat{V}_2)$ be a compensation graph to be obtained after D-deleting rows or columns in G. Then, there is a matching in $\hat{G}$ and there is a closed cycle in each derived connected component $\hat{C}_i$, from which just two different matching in $\hat{C}_i$ are derived. Choose one of them which is denoted as M_i. Let $M = M \bigcup \{\cup_i M_i\}$. Then M is a matching from $\hat{V}_1$ to $\hat{V}_2$.
Step 6: The algorithm ends.   □

The following is the detailed process for executing DRA-OT-DR by hardware, where spare PEs are located in the upper and left sides as shown in Fig. 3.13.

Notation 3.8

- The numbers of unrepaired faulty PEs including a spare in a row r and a column c are denoted as n_f^r and n_f^c, respectively.

(Execution of DRA-OT-DR (shortly written as **EDRA-OT-DR**) for an $X \times Y$ array)

Step I While there is an unrepaired faulty PE in a row or column $*$ with $n_f^* = 1$, do the following (a) and (b) alternatively.

(a) Count the number of unrepaired faulty PEs (including a spare PE) toward a spare in each column. This is done in parallel for all columns. Then, replace a faulty PE in a column c with $n_f^c = 1$ by the spare in the upper side and set n_f^c to 0.

(b) Count the number of unrepaired faulty PEs (including a spare PE) toward a spare in each row. This is done in parallel for all rows. Then, replace a faulty PE in a row r with $n_f^r = 1$ by the spare on the left side and set n_f^r to 0.

Note that a faulty spare is considered to be replaced by itself.

This step corresponds to Step 2 in DRA-OT-DR.

Step II If there is a column or row whose n_f is greater than 2, or equal to 2 and in which a spare is faulty, do the D-deletion process as follows. Otherwise, go to Step IV.

This step corresponds to Step 4 in DRA-OT-DR.

D-deletion process:

Notation:

- r_i $(1 \leq i \leq X)$ denotes the i-th row.
- c_i $(1 \leq i \leq Y)$ denotes the i-th column.
- α is a variable representing a row or column such as r_j or c_j.
- $n_f^{r_i}$ $(n_f^{c_i})$ is the number of unrepaired faulty PEs including the spare in the i-th row (column).
- $\hat{n}_f^{r_i}$ $(\hat{n}_f^{c_i})$ is the number of faults in the i-th row (column) that should be D-deleted to be repaired. They are defined as below.

  Let $R_{F(2)}$ be a set consisting of r_i's such that $n_f^{r_i} \geq 2$ and the spare p_{i0} is faulty. For $r_i \in R_{F(2)}$, $\hat{n}_f^{r_i} = n_f^{r_i} - 1$

  Let $C_{F(2)}$ be a set consisting of c_i's such that $n_f^{c_i} \geq 2$ and the spare p_{0i} is faulty. For $c_i \in C_{F(2)}$, $\hat{n}_f^{c_i} = n_f^{c_i} - 1$.

  Let $R_{F(3)}$ be a set consisting of r_i's where $n_f^{r_i} \geq 3$ and the spare p_{i0} is healthy. For $r_i \in R_{F(3)}$, $\hat{n}_f^{r_i} = n_f^{r_i} - 2$.

  Let $C_{F(3)}$ is a set consisting of c_i's where $n_f^{c_i} \geq 3$ and the spare p_{0i} is healthy. For $c_i \in C_{F(3)}$ $\hat{n}_f^{c_i} = n_f^{c_i} - 2$.

  In the following, $R_{F(2)} \cup R_{F(3)}$ and $C_{F(2)} \cup C_{F(3)}$ are simply denoted as R_F and C_F, respectively.

  If $R_F \cup C_F = \phi$ (i.e., empty), D-deletion process is ended and go to Step IV.

Step III Choose α in $R_F \cup C_F$ and D-delete the row or column corresponding to α, where how to choose α is proposed below. Then go to Step I.

Three methods to choose α are proposed as follows. Note that in executing the process, one method is chosen, which affects the subsequent degradation process and thus the size of a subarray to be obtained.

- Method 1

  Choose α in $R_F \cup C_F$ arbitrarily. In this method, $R_F \cup C_F$ obtained if the n_f's are suppressed to 3 is the same as that by non-suppression. This property is useful in hardware realization to be mentioned in Section 4.
- Method 2

  Choose α in $R_F \cup C_F$ such that $\hat{n}_f^\alpha$ is maximal.
- Method 3

  (1) For each α in $R_F \cup C_F$, the row or column corresponding to α is tried to be D-deleted. Then, let the fault pattern obtained be $P_{D(\alpha)}$.

  (2) Apply Step I to $P_{D(\alpha)}$, compute $R_F' \cup C_F'$ and D-delete the row or column corresponding to α such that $|R_F' \cup C_F'|$ is minimal.

Step IV   A spare PE by which each unrepaired faulty PE in closed cycles in Step 5 in DRA-OT-DR will be replaced is determined.

Step V   The restructuring process with degradation is ended.

□

To help understanding EDRA-OT-DR, Fig. 3.32 is an instance of an 8×8 array with 21 faulty PEs where $\times$'s denote faulty PEs and the arrows are the directions of the compensation for them after Step I in EDRA-OT-DR has been executed. As the result, we have the fault pattern as in Fig. 3.33 in which the black squares are ones which have replaced the faulty PEs shaded with gray. Then, the number of unrepaired faults in each row or column becomes as in Table 3.6. So, $R_{F(2)}=\{r_3, r_6\}$, $R_{F(3)}=\{r_2\}$, $C_{F(2)}=\{c_3\}$ and $C_{F(3)}=\{c_6\}$. By Method 1, α should be chosen arbitrarily. By Method 2, r_6 is chosen as α since $\hat{n}_f^{r_6}$ is maximal. By Method 3, applying (1) and (2) in Method 3, r_6 is chosen since $|R_F' \cup C_F'|$ is 2 and minimal, where $|R_F' \cup C_F'|$'s for r_2, r_3, c_3 and c_6 are 3, 3, 4, and 3, respectively, which can easily be checked.

Now, choosing and D-deleting r_6 in the subarray in Fig. 3.33, Step I in EDRA-OT-DR is applied to the subarray obtained where the arrows in Fig. 3.34 indicate the directions of compensation for the faulty PEs after Step I in EDRA-OT-DR have been executed. Then, the number of unrepaired faults remained in each row or column becomes as in Table 3.7. Then, either r_3 or c_3 can be D-deleted. Here, suppose D-delete c_3. Then, the subarray as in Fig. 3.35 is obtained, $R_F \cup C_F$ is empty, and EDRA-OT-DR is ended. Finally, we have an array restructured with degradation whose size is 7×7 where the arrows in Fig. 3.36 indicate the directions of compensation for the faults and the squares marked with $+$ are PEs D-deleted which are bypassed vertically and horizontally.

We have presented a degradable restructuring algorithm for mesh arrays by direct spare replacement and described how the algorithm is executed.

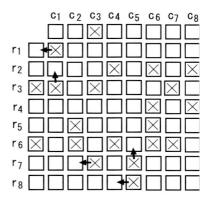

Fig. 3.32 Arrows indicate directions of compensation for faults after Step I in EDRA-OT-DR has been executed

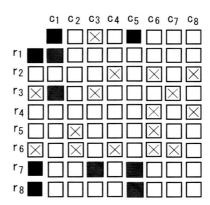

Fig. 3.33 Black squares are spares which have replaced faulty PEs marked with gray

Table 3.6 n_f and $\hat{n}_f$ for Fig. 3.33

i	1	2	3	4	5	6	7	8
$n_f^{r_i}$	0	3	3	2	2	5	0	0
$\hat{n}_f^{r_i}$	–	1	2	–	–	4	–	–
$n_f^{c_i}$	0	2	2	2	0	4	2	2
$\hat{n}_f^{c_i}$	–	–	1	–	–	2	–	–

3.5.2 Evaluation

Several terms and measures to evaluate DRA-OT-DR are introduced as follows.

1. A fault pattern P is called to be $D(r, s)$-repairable if it is restructured by D-deleting r rows and s columns by EDRA-OT-DR.
2. N_a is the number of all PEs for an array with size of $X \times Y$, i.e., $(X + 1) \cdot (Y + 1) - 1$.

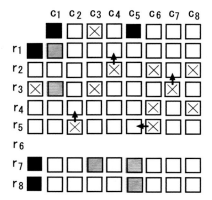

Fig. 3.34 Subarray obtained by D-deleting the 6th row and arrows are directions of compensation for faults after Step I in EDRA-OT-DR has been executed

Table 3.7 n_f and $\hat{n}_f$ for Fig. 3.34

i	1	2	3	4	5	6	7	8
$n_f^{r_i}$	0	2	2	2	0	–	0	0
$\hat{n}_f^{r_i}$	–	–	1	–	–	–	–	–
$n_f^{c_i}$	0	0	2	0	0	2	0	2
$\hat{n}_f^{c_i}$	–	–	1	–	–	–	–	–

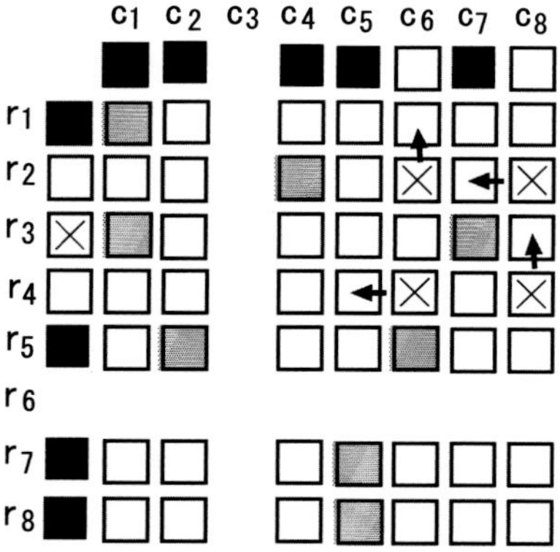

Fig. 3.35 One of subarrays finally obtained by D-deletion

3. $N_e(k)$ is the number of examined fault patterns which have k faulty PEs.
4. $N_{res}(k; r, s)$ is the number of $D(r, s)$-repairable fault patterns which have k faulty PEs.
5. $N_{res}(k; d)$ is the number of $D(r, s)$-repairable examined fault patterns which have k faulty PEs and $d = r + s$, i.e., $N_{res}(k; d) = \sum_{r+s=d} N_{res}(k; r, s)$.
6. D-restructured rate $DRR(k; d)$ is defined as $DRR(k; d) = N_{res}(k; d)/N_e(k)$.

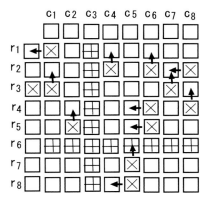

Fig. 3.36 D-restructured array with usable size of 7×7 where faulty PEs and boxes with mark $+$ are bypassed horizontally and vertically

7. $SDRR(k; d)$ is defined as $SDRR(k; d) = \sum_{0 \le i \le d} DRR(k; i)$.
8. Noting that a $D(r, s)$-restructured array is a subarray with size of $(X - r) \times (Y - s)$, we define the average number of usable PEs $AU(k)$ for the number of faulty PEs k, normalized by $(X \cdot Y)$ as follows.

$$AU(k) = 1/(X \cdot Y) \sum_{0 \le r, s} (X - r)(Y - s) \cdot N_{res}(k; r, s)/N_e(k).$$

To evaluate the terms introduced above, we have executed Monte Carlo simulations, using a PC with Borland C++ Compiler 5.5. Here, it is assumed that all the PEs may become uniformly faulty. Then, 10^6 random fault patterns each with k faulty PEs for $1 \le k \le (X + Y)$ are generated (Figs. 3.37 and 3.38).

Figure 3.39 shows $AU(k)$ for the cases that $X=Y=8$, 16 and 32. It is seen that $AU(k)$'s increase in the order of M1, M2, and M3. However, for easiness of hardware realization, Method 1 is adopted in the next section because the differences among them are so small.

3.5.3 Hardware Realization of the Algorithm

The following is the more detailed outline of realizing the above for an $X \times X$ mesh array where the spare PEs are supposed to be located in the upper and left sides of the array as shown in Fig. 3.13.

Notation:

- A faulty PE which is not D-deleted is said to be repaired if it is replaced by a healthy spare PE. A mesh array is said to be repaired without D-deletion if all faulty PEs are repaired without D-deletion.

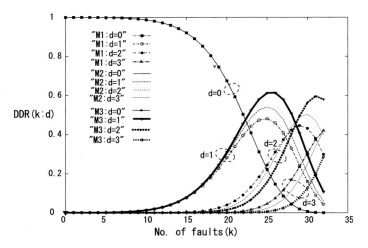

Fig. 3.37 D-restructured rate for arrays with size of 16×16

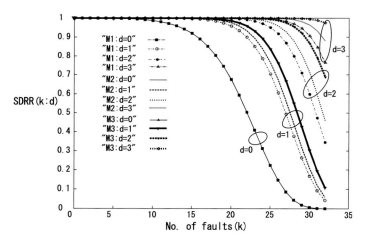

Fig. 3.38 SDRR for arrays with size of 16×16

- The number of unrepaired faulty PEs in a row or column (α) is denoted as n_f^α

  (Detailed outline of hardware realization)

(1). Do the following (a) and (b) X times.

   (a) Count the number of unrepaired faulty PEs (including a spare PE) toward a
   spare in each column. This is done in parallel for all columns. Then, replace a
   faulty PE in a column with $n_f = 1$ by a spare in the upper side and set n_f to 0.
   (b) Count the number of unrepaired faulty PEs (including a spare PE) toward
   a spare in each row. This is done in parallel for all rows. Then, replace a faulty

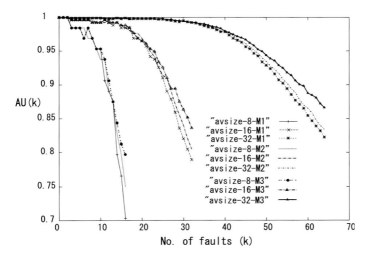

Fig. 3.39 Average sizes for D-deleted arrays with sizes of $X \times Y$ ($X = Y = 8, 16, 32$)

PE in a row with $n_f = 1$ by a spare on the left side and set n_f to 0.
This step corresponds to Step I in EDRA-OT-DR.

(2). (i) If there is a column or row with $n_f \geq 3$ or
(ii) there is a column or row with $n_f = 2$ and the spare in the column or row is
faulty, the array with faults is unrepairable without D-deletion, the signal "1"
indicating so is output from the terminal UNRP and the D-deletion process is
executed once. Then go to 1). Otherwise, go to the next step.
This step corresponds to Step III in EDRA-OT-DR.

(3). The array is repairable and if $n_f = 0$ for all columns and rows, the repairing
process is ended. Otherwise, go to the next step.

(4). A spare PE by which each unrepaired faulty PE in closed cycles in Step 5 in
DRA-OT-DR will be replaced is determined as follows.
This step corresponds to Step IV in EDRA-OT-DR.

To begin with the leftmost column, do the following.

(i) Check whether there are unrepaired faulty PEs in the column. This is done
by sending a signal "1" from the lowest row in the column toward the upper.
If it is confirmed that there is none, go to the column next to the right.
Otherwise, there are unrepaired two faulty PE, s. say PEs A and B, in the
column and A is located in the lower row, and A will receives the signal "1".
Then, A sends the signal "1" to the left and right and is replaced by a spare
PE located on the left side. As a general rule,

- A faulty PE which has received a signal "1" from the upper or lower sends signal the "1" to the right and left, and is replaced by a spare PE located on the left side.
- A faulty PE which has received a signal "1" from the left or right sends the signal "1" to the upper and lower, and is replaced by a spare PE located in the upper side.
- A healthy or repaired PE only passes a signal which it has received.

(ii) Finally, a signal "1" must reach the PE A via PE B. If the column checked is the rightmost column, this process is ended. Otherwise, go to the column next to the right and go to (i). □

First, a logical circuit NET-1 which realizes from (1) to (3) in the detailed outline is shown. Next, NET-2 which decides the directions of replacements for faulty PEs in closed cycle in (4) in the detailed outline is shown.

Figure 3.40 shows the logical circuit NET-1 which consists of modules MPE, MSP, two shift-registers each with the same function and several gates, where SP is a spare PE, MPE is shown in (b), and MSP in (c). The functions of these modules are explained in the following.

Assumption

- Each PE (including spare PE) outputs 1 as it's fault signal if it is faulty, and 0 otherwise. The fault signal of a nonspare PE (spare PE) is input to the terminal F of MPE (MSP) as shown in Fig. 3.40. □

Notation 3.9

- $PE(x, y)$ (including spare PE) denotes the PE in the x-th row and y-th column, where $PE(0,y)$ ($PE(x,0)$) denotes the spare PE on the upper (left) side of an array.
- Input signal to a terminal number n is denoted as i_n. The output signal out of a terminal number m is denoted as o_m.
- $i(x, y)$ and $o(x, y)$ denote the input and output to/from $MPE(x, y)$, where $MPE(0, y)$ ($MPE(x, 0)$) denotes MSP in the y-th column (x-th row).
- $n_f(0, y)$ ($n_f(x, 0)$) denotes the number of unrepaired faulty PEs including the spare PE in the y-th column (x-th row). □

- The function of C_1

C_1 is used to count n_f in a row or a column and check whether $n_f > 2$. To do so, C_1 adds binary numbers $(x_1x_0)_2$ and $(0f)_2$, and outputs a binary number $(y_1y_0)_2$ but the sum is upper-limited to 3, that is, $(11)_2$ if it is greater than 2, as shown in Fig. 3.40a.

Fig. 3.40 NET-1 for
executing Steps 2 to 5 in
DRA-OT-DR

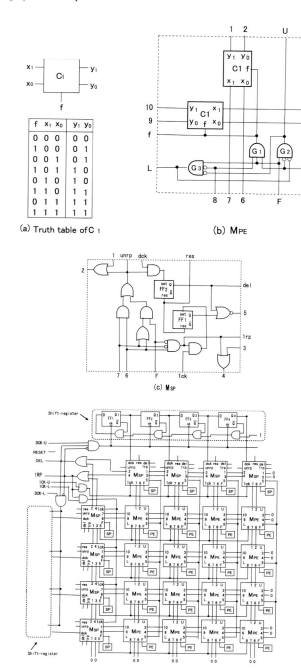

(a) Truth table of C_1

(b) M_{PE}

(c) M_{SP}

Table 3.8 Behavior of G_2 and G_3

i_5^t	i_8^t	o_U^t	o_L^t
0	0	$o_U^{(t-1)}$	$o_L^{(t-1)}$
0	1	1	0
1	0	0	1
1	1	0	0

Table 3.9 Truth table for unrp and 1rp

	F	i_7	i_6	unrp	1rp
(i)	0	0	0	0	0
(ii)	1	0	0	0	0
(iii)	0	0	1	0	1
(iv)	1	0	1	1	0
(v)	0	1	0	0	0
(vi)	1	1	0	1	0
(vii)	0	1	1	1	0
(viii)	1	1	1	1	0

- The function of MPE

  1. If both the signals i_5 and i_8 are 1s (so initially as will be shown in 1) of the behavior of NET-1), $o_f = i_F$, and 0 otherwise.
  2. If $i_F = 1$ (so if the PE is faulty), the outputs o_U^t and o_L^t of the gate G_2 and G_3 at time t are as shown in Table 3.8, according to the signals i_5^t and i_8^t of the terminals 5 and 8 at time t. This means that the combination of G_2 and G_3 works as a flip-flop with the inputs i_5 and i_8.

- The function of MSP

  $o_5 = 1$ if and only if both output of FF$_1$ and FF$_2$ are 0, where FF$_1$ is set to 1 when 1rp = 1ck = 1, and FF$_2$ is set to 1 when unrp = dck = 1. Here, unrp and 1rp are defined by Table 3.9. From Table 3.9, it is seen that 1rp = 1 if and only if i_F=0 and $(i_7 i_6)_2 = 1$, and unrp=1 if and only if ($i_F = 1$ and $(i_7 i_6)_2 \geq 1$) or ($(i_7 i_6)_2 \geq 3$).

  The logical equations of unrp and 1rp are given by

  $$unrp = F \cdot (i_7 + i_6) + i_7 \cdot i_6.$$
  $$1rp = \bar{F} \cdot \bar{i_7} \cdot i_6.$$

- The behavior of circuit NET-1

1. Initially, all the flip-flop FFs in M_{SP}'s and the shift-registers are reset; that is, o_5 and dck of each M_{SP} is 1 and 0, respectively. Then, i_5 and i_8 of each M_{PE} are 1s, and $(i_7 i_6)_2$ of each M_{SP} shows n_f in the row or column though it is upper-limited to 3.

2. The behavior of NET-1 is controlled by the clocks input to the terminals 1CK-U, 1CK-L, DCK-U. and DCK-L. They are fed as follows, which is called D-process.
   D-process:
   (i) While 1RP=1, 1CK-U and 1CK-L are fed alternatively as $1ck$-$u(1)$, $1ck$-$\ell(1)$, $1ck$-$u(2)$, $1ck$-$\ell(2)$, ... where $1ck$-$u(i)$ and $1ck$-$\ell(i)$ are the i-th clocks to 1CK-U and 1CK-L, respectively.
   (ii) If UNRP $= 0$ then D-process is ended. Otherwise DCK-U is fed. Then, if 1RP becomes 1, while 1RP $= 1$, 1CK-U and 1CK-L are fed alternatively.
   (iii) If UNRP $= 0$ then D-process is ended. Otherwise DCK-L is fed. Then, if 1RP becomes 1, while 1RP $= 1$, 1CK-U and 1CK-L are fed alternatively as in (i).
   (iv) If 1RP becomes 0, go to (ii).

3. If 1RP $= 1$, there is an M_{SP} whose output o_{1rp} is 1. When 1RP=1 and a clock through 1CK-U is input to 1ck of M_{SP} ($= M_{PE(0, y)}$), if 1rp from the M_{SP} is 1, i.e., PE(0, y) is healthy and $n_f(0, y) = 1$, FF_1 of the M_{SP} is set to 1 and $o_5(0, y)$ becomes 0. Then, o_U of $M_{PE(x, y)}$ such that PE(x, y) is faulty becomes 1. This indicates that the faulty PE(x, y) is replaced by the spare PE in the y-th column. Further, o_U's and o_L's of all the other M_{PE}'s in the y-th column become 0's because i_F of the other M_{PE}'s in the y-th column are 0's, $i_5 = 0$ and $i_8 = 1$.

4. When a clock through 1CK-L is input, the similar move to that in 3 above is performed where "column" is replaced by "row".

5. DEL $= 1$ if and only if unrp of some M_{SP} is 1 if and only if $n_f \geq 3$ or ($n_f = 2$ including a faulty spare) in a row or a column. Hence, DEL $= 1$ of NET-1 indicates that the array with the faults is irreparable without D-deletion.

6. If DEL $= 0$, unrp's of all M_{SP}'s are 0's, which indicates that the array with the faults is repairable. Then, if there is neither row nor column such that $n_f = 2$, the spare is healthy and o_5 of M_{SP} is 1, this repairing D-process can be successfully ended with or without D-process. Then go to the process for finding closed cycles (even if there may not be such cycles) together with the directions of replacing for faulty PEs in the cycles. This process corresponds to (4) in the detailed outline and is executed by NET-2 shown in Fig. 3.42.

- The function of M+

1. The terminal f of M_{PE} in NET-1 is connected to the terminal F of M+.
2. If i_F ($= o_f$) is 0, the internal structure becomes as shown in Fig. 3.42b, i.e., the signals pass through horizontally and vertically.
3. If $i_F = 1$, the internal structure becomes as Fig. 3.42a. Then,
   (i) (a) the signal through x_3 from the top or (b) x_1 from the bottom are transferred to the left through y_4 and the right through y_2, and the signal is stored in the

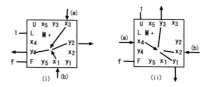

Fig. 3.41 Signal flow of inputs and outputs when $i_F = 1$

flip-flop FF$_L$ which indicates that the direction of replacement is to the left. This scene is seen in Fig. 3.41(i).

(ii) (a) The signal through x_4 from the left or (b) x_2 from the right are transferred to the lower through y_1 and the upper through y_3, and the signal is stored in the flip-flop FF$_U$ which indicates that the direction of replacement is to the upper. This scene is seen in Fig. 3.41(ii).

- The behavior of circuit NET-2

Note that (i) the internal structure of M$_+$ becomes as Fig. 3.42b if a PE with the M$_+$ is healthy or has been repaired and in (a) if it has not yet been repaired, and (ii) there are exactly two unrepaired faulty PEs in a row or column in a closed cycle.

1. Initially, all the flip-flops are reset.
2. Signal "1" is shifted from the left to the right in the shift-register at the time when the output of G$_1$ is 0 and a clock pulse is fed to CLK-1.
3. Increasing i from 1 to X, the following is performed.
   (i) A clock is fed to all the flip-flops in Fig. 3.42 through CLK-2 except ones in the shift-register.
   (ii) If Q_i of the shift-register becomes 1, this signal "1" is input to x_1 of M$_+$ in the bottom row of i-th column. At the time, the output of the gate G$_1$ becomes 1 and hence a clock to CLK-1 is inhibited to be supplied to the shift register. While a clock to CLK-1 is not supplied, the signal "1" input to the i-th column behaves as follows.

   - If there is no unrepaired faulty PE in the i-th column, the signal "1" passes through all the M$_+$s in the column, turns back at the M$_+$ in the top row of the column (note that the terminals x_5 and y_3 are connected) and reaches the terminal y_5 of the M$_+$ in the bottom row of the column.
   - If there are unrepaired faulty PEs, there are exactly two such PEs in the column whose M$_+$s are denoted as M$_+^L$ and M$_+^U$ where the former is in a lower location. The signal "1" is fed to M$_+^L$ and propagates in a closed cycle as mentioned in (4) in the detailed outline of hardware realization, finally reaches M$_+^U$, sent in the upper direction, turn back at M$_+$ in the top row and reaches the terminal y_5 of the M$_+$ in the bottom row of the column.
   - The signal "1" which reaches y_5 of the M$_+$ in the bottom row as above is memorized in the D-FF by a clock to CLK-2 and fed to the gate G$_2$. Then,

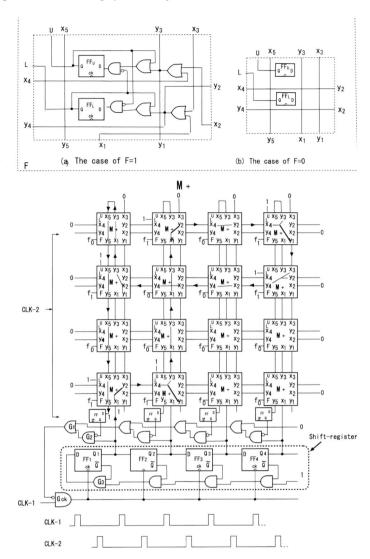

Fig. 3.42 NET-2 for deciding the directions of replacement while executing Step 6 in DRA-OT-DR

the outputs of G_2 and G_1 become 0s, and hence, a clock to CLK-1 can pass through the gate G_{ck}.

The above should be seen as an instance in Fig. 3.42 in which the arrows show the flow of the signal "1".

From the explanation so far, it is seen that NET-1 and NET-2 exactly execute each step in EDRA-OT-DR.

3.6 Degradable Restructuring by STS

An algorithm modified a little from RA-OT-STS is applied to an array, rotating
spare locations around the array. The algorithm that if the array does not satisfy the
repairable condition, its rows and/or columns are functionally deleted so that the
subarray with the remaining rows and columns satisfies the repairable condition is
presented. The restructuring effect is evaluated from three terms. Finally, a hardware
to realize the algorithm is briefly described.

Before giving a degradable restructuring algorithm, we present an algorithm modified a little from RA-OT-STS which is denoted as mRA-OT-STS.

Notation 3.10

- $D = (d_{ij})$ and $S = (s_{ij})$ are matrices with the same size as that of a fault pattern
  $P = (p_{ij})$.
- $R = (r_i)$ and $C = (c_i)$ are matrices consisting of variables r_i's and c_i's ($\leq i \leq N$),
  respectively, .
- flg is a flag.
- sum is a variable.   □

mRA-OT-STS

begin

Step 0. Setting

Step 0-1: Set d_{ij} to 0 for all i, j ($0 \leq i \leq N$), ($0 \leq j \leq N$)
Step 0-2: Set sfg to 1.
Step 0-3: Set all the elements of S to 1's
Step 0-4: Set all the elements of R and C to 0's

Step 1: Decreasing j from N to 1 do

Step 1-1: Set flg to p_{0j};
Step 1-2: Increasing i from 1 to N do
Step 1-2-1: If $d_{ij} = 2$ then set flg to 1;
Step 1-2-2: If ($p_{ij} = 1$ and $flg=1$) then do
Step 1-2-2-1: set d_{ij} to 2
Step 1-2-2-2: Decreasing k from $j - 1$ to 0 do
Step 1-2-2-2-1: if $p_{ik} = 1$ then do

set s_{ik} to 0
set d_{ik} to 3
increase r_i by 1
increase c_k by 1

Step 1-2-2-2-2: else set d_{ik} to 2
    Step 1-3: if ($p_{ij} = 1$ and $flg=0$) then do
  Step 1-3-1: Set flg to 1
  Step 1-3-2: Decreasing k from i to 0 do
 Step 1-3-2-1: Set d_{kj} to 1;

 Step 2: set sum to 0
 Step 3: Increasing i from 1 to N do

Step 3-1: increase sum by r_i

end

⬚

We have the following property for repairability

Property 3.15 *An array of physical size* $(N + 1) \times (N + 1)$ *with a fault pattern* $P = (p_{ij})$ *can be repaired into an array with logical size* $N \times N$ *(in the meaning of Property 2.3) if and only if mRA-OT-STS ends returning sum* $= 0$. ⬚

The following are an instance of a fault pattern for a $(8+1)\times(8+1)$ PA and the D-matrix derived by executing mRA-OT-STS.

$$
\begin{array}{ccccccccc}
0 & 1 & 0 & 0 & 0 & 0 & 0 & 0 & 0 \\
1 & 0 & 0 & 0 & 0 & 0 & 1 & 0 & 1 \\
0 & 0 & 0 & 0 & 0 & 0 & 0 & 1 & 1 \\
0 & 1 & 0 & 1 & 0 & 0 & 0 & 1 & 1 \\
0 & 0 & 0 & 0 & 0 & 1 & 0 & 0 & 0 \\
0 & 1 & 0 & 0 & 1 & 0 & 0 & 0 & 0 \\
0 & 0 & 0 & 0 & 0 & 0 & 0 & 0 & 0 \\
0 & 0 & 0 & 0 & 0 & 0 & 0 & 1 & 0 \\
1 & 0 & 0 & 1 & 0 & 0 & 0 & 0 & 0 \\
\end{array}
$$

(i) An instance of a fault pattern

```
0 0 0 0 0 0 1 1 1
0 0 0 0 0 0 1 1 1
2 2 2 2 2 2 2 3 2
2 3 2 3 2 2 2 3 2
2 2 2 2 2 2 0 0 0
2 3 2 2 2 0 0 0 0
0 0 0 0 0 0 0 0 0
2 2 2 2 2 2 2 2 0
3 2 2 2 0 0 0 0 0
```

(ii) D-matrix derived after mRA-OT-STS has been executed

i	0	1	2	3	4	5	6	7	8
r_i	0	0	1	3	0	1	0	0	1
c_i	1	2	0	1	0	0	0	2	0

(iii) The number of 3s in each row and column

From the above, $sum = 6$.
Now, we present a degradable restructuring algorithm.

3.6.1 Degradable Restructuring Algorithm (DRA-OT-STS)

The degradation of an array is done by functionally (or logically) deleting rows and/or columns of the array so that sum is decreased and finally becomes zero. Then, the problem arises: which rows and/or columns should be deleted? Here, we propose the following algorithm DRA-OT-STS.

In the following, D-deleting rows and columns of an array with a fault pattern P is used in the same meaning as setting the rows and columns of P to 0's, if no confusion occurs.

DRA-OT-STS

- P is a fault pattern with a size of $(N + 1) \times (N + 1)$.
- G is a matrix with the same size as that of P.
- $R = \{r(i)|1 \leq i \leq N\}$ (a set of rows) and $C = \{c(i)|1 \leq i \leq N\}$ (a set of columns).
- G_α is the pattern (matrix) obtained by D-deleting $\alpha \in R \cup C$ in G.

Step I $G = P$ (i.e., copy P to G).
Step II Apply mRA-OT-STS to G.
         If $sum = 0$, the algorithm successfully ends. Otherwise, go to the next step
Step III Two methods to choose α are proposed as follows. Note that in executing
         the process, one method is chosen and fixed.
         • Method 1 (also called **min-method**)
         (1) Set i to 1.
         (2) Let $G_{r(i)}$ and $G_{c(i)}$ be the patterns (matrices) obtained by D-deleting the
         i-th row and i-th column of G, respectively. Apply mRA-OT-STS to $G_{r(i)}$
         and $G_{c(i)}$, respectively. Let $sum_{r(i)}$ and $sum_{c(i)}$ be the sum's returned from
         mRA-OT-STS.
         If $sum_{r(i)} = 0$, the algorithm ends with degraded pattern $G_{r(i)}$.
         If $sum_{c(i)} = 0$, the algorithm ends with degraded pattern $G_{c(i)}$.
         (3) If $i < N$, increase i by 1 and go to (2) .
         (4) If $i = N$, compute $min = Min_{1 \leq i \leq N} \{sum_{r(i)}, sum_{c(i)}\}$ and let i_{min} be
         the index such that $min = sum_{*(i_{min})}$ ($*$ is either r or c). Set $G = G_{*(i_{min})}$ and
         goto (1).
         • Method 2 (also called **max-method**)
         (i) Choose $\alpha \in R \cup C$ such that sum_α is maximal. Set $G = G_\alpha$.
         (ii) Apply mRA-OT-STS to G. If $sum = 0$, the algorithm ends, otherwise
         goto (i).   □

If DRA-OT-STS ends with $sum = 0$, the subarray according to G obtained by
D-deleting the rows and columns is repairable, and P is called **D(r, s)-repairable**
if it is restructured by D-deleting r rows and s columns. Then, it is seen that the
subarray can be used as the array with a size of $(N - r) \times (N - s)$ from Property
3.15.

3.6.2 Applying Orthogonal-Side-Rotation Method

First, mRA-OT-STS is applied to an array modified according to each of the four
assignments mentioned above where the modification is defined as in Eq. 3.6. Then,
each of the modified mRA-OT-STSs is applied at a time to an array with faults and
if at least one of them ends with $sum = 0$, the array with faulty PEs is judged to be
repairable and the array is called to be **DROT-repairable**.
    Instead of the above, one to fix the spares on one of the four orthogonal sides is
called nonROT method.
    DRA-OT-STS is performed using ROT method, which is denoted as **DRA-OT-
STS(ROT)**.

3.6.3   *Evaluation*

DRA-OT-STS and DRA-OT-STS(ROT) are evaluated in terms defined in the Sect. 3.5.2.

Monte Carlo simulations have been executed, using a PC with Borland C++ Compiler 5.5. Here, it is assumed that all the PEs may become uniformly faulty. Then, 10^4 random fault patterns each with k faulty PEs for $1 \leq k \leq X = Y$ are generated provided that each PE in an array may be faulty with the equal reliability.

Figures 3.43 and 3.44 show $DRR(k; d)$ and $SDRR(k; d)$ for arrays with size of 16×16, respectively, where "min" and "rot" correspond to the cases that min- and ROT methods are applied, respectively.

Figure 3.45 shows $AU(k)$ for the cases that $N = 8$, 16 and 32. It is seen that $AU(k)$'s increase in the order of "max", "min", and "rot-min".

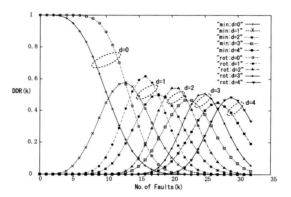

Fig. 3.43   D-restructured rate for arrays with sized of 16×16

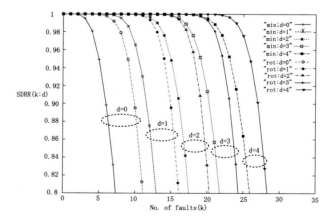

Fig. 3.44   SDRR for arrays with size of 16×16

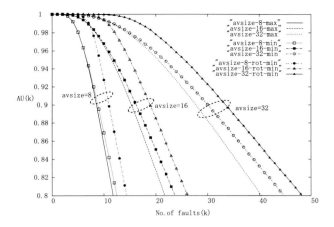

Fig. 3.45 Average sizes for D-deleted arrays with sizes of N×N (N = 8, 16, 32)

3.6.4 Hardware Realization of the Algorithm

Though two methods, i.e., min-method and max-method, have been proposed, here the hardware realization of the former will be briefly explained through Fig. 3.46.

Figure 3.46 shows a hardware realization of mRA-OT-STS. Each PE has a logical circuit CC (CC_D or CC_U) shown in Fig. 3.46a or b, which is connected as shown in the figure, along with the signals to and from the CCs. The CC has the input signals f, D_{in}, L_{in}, U_{in}, f and a_i, and the output signals D_{out}, L_{out}, U_{out} and a_o. The signal f's correspond to p_{ij}'s in mRA-OT-STS, D_{in}'s to flg's, L_{out}'s to 2-sequences, U_{out}'s to 1-sequences, respectively, and $\overline{S}_g$ corresponds to s_{ik}. Then, In order to switch the connections among PEs correctly, it is necessary and sufficient to know the correspondences between 1- or 2-sequences and the signals in the circuit which are stated in Properties 3.17 and 3.18. Further, using the circuits consisting of "control", "min-det", shift register, and some additional parts, the functional deletion of row $r(x)$ or column $c(y)$ is done by setting $d_{gr}(x, 0)$ or $d_{gc}(0, y)$ to 0's for ($0 \leq x$, $y \leq N$), where x or y is identified from that the output 'sum' from CC at the left- and upper-most corner which is minimal.

Here, the signals are defined by the equations below.

$$D_{out} = p + D_{in} + L_{in} \tag{3.7}$$

$$L_{out} = L_{in} + p \cdot D_{in} \tag{3.8}$$

$$U_{out} = U_{in} + p \cdot \overline{D}_{in} \tag{3.9}$$

$$\overline{S}_g = p \cdot L_{in} \tag{3.10}$$

$$a_0 = \text{Add}(a_i, \overline{S}_g) \tag{3.11}$$

From the equations above, we can see that the logical circuit of a CC is simple.

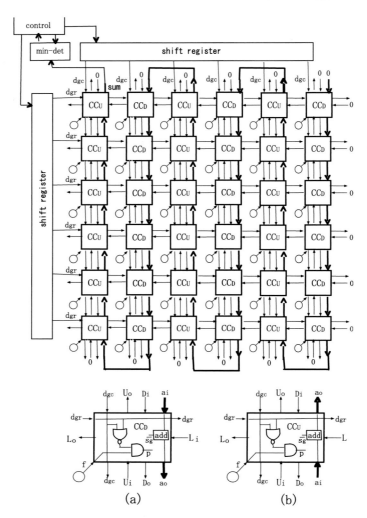

Fig. 3.46 CC network to realize mRA-OT-STS where Input and output signals of control circuit CC

It could be proved similarly as in [4] that the behavior of the CC network shown in Fig. 3.46 is compatible with that of mRA-OT-STS (see Properties 3.16, 3.17 and 3.18). Property 3.16 is used to check whether an array with faulty PEs is repairable or not. Property 3.17 shows the correspondence between 2-sequences and sequences of L_{out}'s. Property 3.18 shows the correspondence between 1-sequences and sequences of U_{out}'s.

Property 3.16 *An array with faulty PEs is repairable, that is, the repairability condition for OT-STS (Property 3.10) is satisfied if and only if the output signal sum input to the min-det is 0.*					□

When $sum = 0$ is output, switching the connections among PEs is done as in Sect. 3.4 from Properties 3.17 and 3.18.

Property 3.17 $d_{xy} = 2$ *if and only if* $L_{out}(x, y) = 1.$					□

Property 3.18 $d_{xy} = 1$ *if and only if* $U_{out}(x, y) = 1.$					□

It has been seen that the ROT method has the highest efficiency. DRA-OT-STS(ROT) will be realized by adding the circuits in Sect. 3.4.4 to the circuits in Fig. 3.46. The details are omitted.

References

1. Takanami, I., Horita, T.: A built-in self-reconfigurable scheme for 3D mesh arrays. IEICE Trans. Inf. Syst. **E82-D**(12), 1554–1562 (1999).
2. Takanami, I., et al.: A built-in self-repair circuit for restructuring mesh-connected processor arrays by direct spare replacement. Trans. Comput. Sci. XXVII, LNCS **9570**, 97–119 (2016)
3. Kung, S.Y., Jean, S.N., Chang, C.W.: Fault-tolerant array processors using single-track switches. IEEE Trans. Comput. **38**(4), 501–514 (1989)
4. Takanami, I.: Self-reconfiguring of $\frac{1}{2}$-track-switch mesh arrays with spares on one row and one column by simple built-in circuit. IEICE. Trans. Inf. Syst. **E87-D**(10), 2318–2328 (2004)
5. Takanami, I., Fukushi, M., Watanabe, T.: Self-restructuring of mesh connected processor arrays with spares assigned on rotated orthogonal side. Trans. Comput. Sci. **XXXVIII**, 36–53 (2021). Springer
6. Kuo, S.Y., Chen, I.Y.: Efficinet reconfiguration algorithms for degradable VLSI/WSI arrays. IEEE Trans. Comput.-Aided Design **11**(10), 1289–1300 (1992)
7. Low, C.P., Leong, H.W.: On the reconfiguration of degradable VLSI/WSI arrays. IEEE Trans. Comput.-Aided Design Integr. Circuits Syst. **16**(10), 1213–1221 (1997)
8. Fukushi, M., Fukushima, Y., Horiguchi, S.: A genetic approach for the reconfiguration of degradable processor arrays. In: IEEE 20th International Symposium on Defect and Fault Tolerance in VLSI Systems, pp. 63–71 (2005)
9. Fukushima, Y., Fukushi, M., Horiguchi, S.: An improved reconfiguration method for degradable processor arrays using genetic algorithm. In: IEEE 21st International Symposium on Defect and Fault Tolerance in VLSI Systems, pp. 353–361 (2006)
10. Takanami, I., Fukushi, M.: Degradable self-restructuring of mesh connected processor arrays by direct spare replacement. Trans. Comput. Sci. **XXXIX**, 1–21 (2022). Springer

Chapter 4
2D Arrays with 3N Spares

Abstract An array with spares on three sides is treated. The array with faults is restructured using STS. A method to divide the array into two subarrays and apply ROT method to each subarray is described. The survival rates and array reliabilities are shown.

Keywords Fault-tolerance · Two-dimensional array · Spares on three sides · Restructuring · Reconfiguration · Single-track-shift · Built-in circuit · Spare rotation

4.1 Spare Arrangement and Restructuring Algorithm

Figure 4.1 shows an array with spares on three sides. Here, it will be adopted that a faulty PE is compensated for by a spare on the same row or column using STS. Then, a method to divide an array into two subarrays as shown in Fig. 4.2, and apply ROT method to each subarray will be described (Fig. 4.3).

4.2 Array Reliabilities

Figures 4.4 and 4.5 show the reliabilities in terms of "nonrot", "rot-fix", and "rot-var" where
   "nonrot" corresponds to the case that an array is divided in the center but ROT method is not applied to it.
   "rot-fix" corresponds to the case that an array is divided in the center and ROT method is applied to each of two subarrays independently and the array is judged to be repairable if the subarrays are repairable in at least one pair of rotations.
   "rot-var" corresponds to the case that the dividing line is moved on the left and right, and ROT method is applied to each divided subarrays and the array is judged

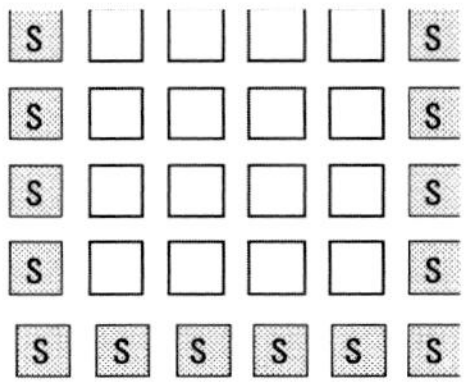

Fig. 4.1 An array with
spares on three sides

Fig. 4.2 An array is divided
in the left and right by a
vertical line

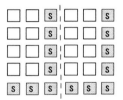

Fig. 4.3 An illustration that
the spare assignment in the
left subarray is rotated by
180°

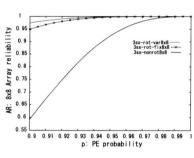

Fig. 4.4 Reliabilities of
arrays with size of 8 × 8

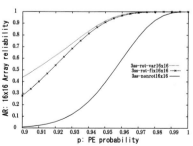

Fig. 4.5 Reliabilities of
arrays with size of 16 × 16

to be repairable if the subarrays are repairable in at least one moved division and a
pair of rotations.

Chapter 5
Two-Dimensional Arrays with 4N Spares

Abstract An algorithm for restructuring 2D-arrays with faults which have spares around them is described. It divides the arrays into four subarrays such that each subarray has spares on the orthogonal two sides. Then, ROT method is applied to each subarray. The method varying the dividing positions is also described. It is shown that the array reliabilities for the proposed method increase so much, comparing with that for non-dividing method as in [1]. A hardware realization of the algorithm with ROT method is described.

Keywords Fault-tolerance · Two-dimensional array · Spares on four sides · Restructuring · Reconfiguration · Single-track-shift · Built-in circuit · Spare rotation

5.1 Restructuring by Dividing Arrays with ROT Method

5.1.1 Fixed Divide Case

The method is to divide a PA into four subarrays and apply ROT-OT-STS to each subarray.

For example, an $(N + 2) \times (N + 2)$ array with spares on the four sides shown in Fig. 5.1 is divided into four subarrays as shown in Fig. 5.2, each with the size of $(\frac{N}{2}+1) \times (\frac{N}{2}+1)$. RA-OT-STS is applied to each subarray, where the $(N + 2) \times (N + 2)$ array (denoted shortly as 4ss-array) has $4(N + 1)$ spares. Then, a 4ss-array with faulty PEs is judged to be repairable if and only if all the subarrays are repairable by ROT-OT-STS. Then, array reliability (AR) of the 4ss-array is calculated by the 4-th power of that of the subarray. Figure 5.5 shows the case of $N = 16$, comparing the ARs of the arrays in OT-STS or ROT method with that of an array with $4N$ spares proposed by Kung et al. [1], where the formers are denoted as 4ss-fixdiv-nonrot and 4ss-fixdiv-fullrot and the latter as Kung(exhaustive) and Kung(neural) [2]. It is seen that the 4ss-fixdiv-fullrot is fairly larger than the Kung, which is so interesting. Further, while ROT method can be realized in a simple hardware, a hardware realization for the

© The Author(s), under exclusive license to Springer Nature Singapore Pte Ltd. 2025
I. Takanami, *Self-restructuring in Fault Tolerant Architecture*,
SpringerBriefs in Computer Science, https://doi.org/10.1007/978-981-96-1539-1_5

Fig. 5.1 An array with
spares on four sides

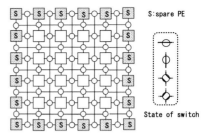

Fig. 5.2 4ss-array divided
into four subarrays

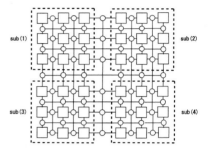

algorithm given by Kung et al. [1] has not yet been shown as far as we know. This
seems to be due to that their algorithm is too complicated to be realized in hardware.
In Fig. 5.5, the curve labeled 4ss-vardiv-fullrot will be mentioned in the following
variable divide case.

To realize ROT method in hardware, it must be shown that subarrays neighboring
with each other after rotations can be connected, keeping the neighboring relation
among logical addresses, by switching sw's, where spares assigned are allowed to
be passed. Figure 5.3 shows an illustration of connections between the cases that
the subarrays of Rot-0 and Rot-180 are adjacent to each other. It is easily seen that
the connections are surely done, keeping the neighboring relation among logical
addresses. Note that unused spare PEs are allowed to be passed vertically and horizontally, using internal switches, as commonly assumed in the existing methods. It
could also be shown that the connections between other Rot-α cases can surely be
done, but it is omitted to illustrate them because it is a simple but tedious task.

5.1.2   Variable Divide Case

We will further discuss the case that a 4ss-array is variably divided into four subarrays,
i.e., row and column positions to be divided are variable. To simulate the case,
RA-OT-STS is modified as follows.

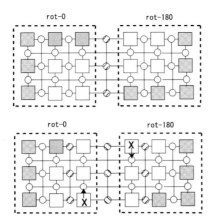

Fig. 5.3 Connections among subarrays of 4ss-array divided into four subarrays. The upper and lower are the cases without failure and with failure between Rot-0 and Rot-180, respectively

Table 5.1 The parameters b_1, b_2, a_{11}, ..., a_{22}, M, N for the rotation

	b_1	b_2	a_{11}	a_{12}	a_{21}	a_{22}	M	N
Rot-0	x_0	y_0	1	0	0	1	x_1-x_0	y_1-y_0
Rot-90	x_0	y_1	0	1	-1	0	y_1-y_0	x_1-x_0
Rot-180	x_1	y_1	-1	0	0	-1	x_1-x_0	y_1-y_0
Rot-270	x_1	y_0	0	-1	1	0	y_1-y_0	x_1-x_0

Let the physical addresses at the top and leftmost, and the bottom and rightmost be (x_0, y_0) and (x_1, y_1) $(x_0 \leq x_1, y_0 \leq y_1)$, respectively. When RA-OT-STS is applied to this subarray, the coordinate transformations for RA-OT-STS are done in accordance with the parameters in Table 5.1 as in Eq. 3.6, and p_{ij} and d_{ij} are replaced by p_{xy} and d_{xy}, respectively. Further M and N in RA-OT-STS are substituted by the parameters in Table 5.1.

Figure 5.4 shows the ex-CC network for a 4ss-array which is modified so that the array to be restructured can be divided at arbitrary row and column positions (refer to Fig. 3.28 about how to switch sw's to input 0s on the sides of ex-CCs). Then, the array is judged to be repairable if all the subarrays are R-repairable at some row and column positions divided. This method is denoted as varROT method. Figure 5.4 illustrates the case that the array is divided between the third and fourth rows and between the fourth and fifth columns.

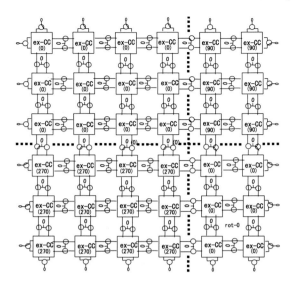

Fig. 5.4 4ss-array variably divided into four subarrays

5.2   Array Reliabilities

The label "4ss-vardiv-fullrot" in Fig. 5.5 shows the AR of the array with size of 16×16 where "4ss-fixdiv fullrot" corresponds to the fixed divide case. 4ss-Kung and 4ss-Kung(neural) are by an exhaustive algorithm and a neural algorithm (refer to [2] and also 6.2) without dividing arrays. From the figure, though the additional sw's

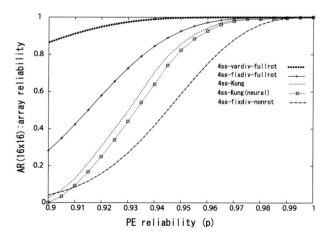

Fig. 5.5 Reliabilities of 4ss-arrays with size of 16×16

and a switch control scheme are needed, it is seen that the ARs by ROT methods increase, and extremely so by varROT method.

References

1. Kung, S.Y., Jean, S.N., Chang, C.W.: Fault-tolerant array processors using single-track switches. IEEE Trans. Comput. **38**(4), 501–514 (1989)
2. Horita, T., Takanami, I.: A built-in self-reconfiguration approach for partitioned mesh-arrays using neural algorithm. IEICE Trans. Inf. Syst. **E79-D**(8), 1160–1167 (1996)

Chapter 6
Three Dimensional Arrays

Abstract A three-dimensional array (3D array) consists of processors (PEs) connected to each other in three dimensions. Two models for restructuring 3D arrays with faults by single-track shifting toward spares are described. One has spares on two opposite surfaces on an array and another has spares on the six surfaces. A restructuring algorithm for each model is given, which can be performed by hardware with switches around each PE. By computer simulation, the survival rates and the reliabilities of arrays which indicate the effectiveness of restructuring are shown.

Keywords Fault-tolerance · Three dimensional arrays · Spares on six surfaces · Spares on two opposite surfaces · Restructuring · Reconfiguration · Single-track shift · Neural algorithm

3D mesh architectures offer a greater degree of interconnection as compared to 2D meshes. In addition, for meshes with practical sizes, the diameter of a 3D mesh is smaller than that of a 2D mesh since the diameters of the 3D and 2D meshes with N processors are $3N^{\frac{1}{3}}$ and $2N^{\frac{1}{2}}$, respectively. Moreover, due to the rich connectivity that the 3D offers, it seems to be ideal for 3D image processing tasks. Recently, the interest in implementing a parallel computer system in three dimensions (3D) using wafer system integration was considered in [1]. In construction of 3D mesh processor arrays with large sizes, especially by wafer scale integration, there is the possibility of low yield and/or reliability of the system if there is no strategy for coping with defects and faults.[1]

To overcome faults in 2D mesh-connected processor arrays, a number of restructuring schemes have been studied in the literature, e.g., [3–8]. However, as far as we know, there are a few studies for 3D mesh-connected processor arrays. A.Chandra and R.Melhem studied a repairability in the 3D meshes which has spare processors on the six surfaces by extending the $1\frac{1}{2}$-track switch model [4] used in 2D to 3D [1] where it has such advantages that the overhead of hardware is a little because additional networks of tracks and switches are simple and distances between logically

---

[1] The content in this subsection is written, based on the content in the paper [2] (Copyright(C)2022) published from IEICE.

© The Author(s), under exclusive license to Springer Nature Singapore Pte Ltd. 2025   97
I. Takanami, *Self-restructuring in Fault Tolerant Architecture*,
SpringerBriefs in Computer Science, https://doi.org/10.1007/978-981-96-1539-1_6

adjacent PEs are bounded by a small constant. They characterized the repairability condition as the selection problem of the maximal set of independent vertices in graph theory. But it is well known that the solution to the maximum independent set problem is in general NP-complete. On the other hand, it is known that the repairability problem for the $1\frac{1}{2}$-track switch model in 2D can be solved in a polynomial time [5], but it has not yet been proved whether the repairability problem for 3D can be solved in polynomial time. So, first, we will propose a simple model for fault tolerant 3D PAs with spare PEs on the two opposite surfaces of a 3D array. Next, the case with spare PEs on the six surfaces which is the architecture proposed by A.Chandra and R.Melhemon will be treated.

6.1 Spares on Opposite Faces

The fault compensation process is performed by shifting processors on a continuous straight line from a faulty processor to a spare on the surfaces. That is, only two opposite directions in the 3D mesh are allowed for compensation paths, provided that no compensation paths must be in the near-miss relation [4]. Then, the switches with only 4 states can preserve the 3D mesh topology after restructuring for compensating for faults while the architecture proposed by A.Chandra and R.Melhem has spare processors on the six surfaces and uses switches each with 13 states. This implies that this network for restructuring has much less hardware overhead than theirs. Then, first, we give an algorithm in a convenient form for restructuring by hardware the 3D mesh arrays with faults. The algorithm can restructure the 3D mesh arrays in polynomial time. Next, we show the survival rates and the reliabilities (or yields) of the meshes by computer simulation. The reliabilities are compared with those of the model using double tracks for which the near-miss relation among compensation paths is allowed. Second, we design a logical circuit for hardware realization of the algorithm.

6.1.1 Architecture

The 3D mesh architecture can be considered as layers (in the XY plane) of 2D meshes stacked in the direction of Z-axis. A $3 \times 3 \times 3$ mesh is shown in Fig. 6.1. Each processor element (PE) is connected to its six nearest neighbors which are in the X_+, X_-, Y_+, Y_-, Z_+ and Z_- directions.

To augment a 3D mesh into the 3D fault tolerant model, a single track and a four port switch are laid between a PE and each of its four neighbors in the Y_+, Y_-, Z_+ and Z_- directions as shown in Fig. 6.2a. The entire 3D array with size of $N \times N \times N$ is sandwiched between two sides of the X_+ and X_- directions by 2D $N \times N$ layers of spare PEs as shown in Fig. 6.2b. Each switch takes only four states as shown in Fig. 6.3b.

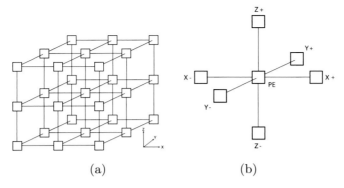

Fig. 6.1 **a** 3 × 3 × 3 mesh array, **b** The six neighbors of a PE

Fig. 6.2 A 3D mesh array
with spares on the opposite
surfaces

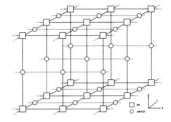

(a)Interconnection of PEs and switches.

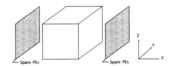

(b) Spare PE's on the grey planes.

6.1.2 Restructuring Algorithm

For the restructuring, we assume that

1. faulty PEs are converted into elements connecting its two ports in the X_+ and X_- directions, and
2. the switching elements and the interconnection wiring are fault-free.

The restructuring strategy is as follows. If a nonspare PE at physical location (x, y, z) is faulty, it may be replaced by its adjacent healthy PE, say at physical location (x', y, z), which in turn will be replaced by the next adjacent healthy PE, say at physical location (x'', y, z), and so on. This replacement process will terminate when a healthy spare PE is used in the end. The process defines a compensation path (in short, c-path). Note that c-paths are straight and continuous.

Fig. 6.3 a An illustration of
compensating for a faulty
PE, **b** Switch state

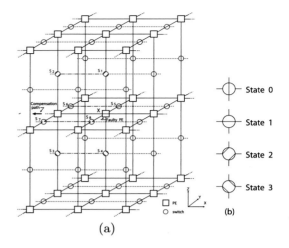

(a)

For each faulty nonspare PE(x, y, z) with physical location (x, y, z), there are
two straight candidate c-paths which go to the X_- and X_+ directions. However, if
there is another faulty PE including a faulty spare PE on a compensation path, it is
not regarded as a candidate c-path. Then, to decide whether a given fault pattern is
repairable or not by using the concept of c-path, we have the following repairability
condition.

Property 6.1 (repairability condition) Given an array of physical size $(N + 2) \times N \times N$, it is repairable into an array of logical size $N \times N \times N$ if

1. we can choose a continuous and straight c-path for each faulty nonspare PE,
2. there is no "near-miss" among the c-paths chosen.   □

Though it is left to give a restructuring algorithm satisfying the statement of
Property 6.1 and its hardware realiztion, it will be omitted since it could be described
by extending RA-OP-STS and the hardware realization for 2D case in Sects. 3.1.1
and 3.1.2 to for 3D case.

6.1.3 Survival Rates and Array Reliabilities

Figure 6.4 shows the survival rates (SV) for the normalized fault number (NFN)
where $NFN(k) = \frac{k}{N_s}$ for the numbers of spare PEs $N_s = 2N^2$ and the number of
faults k. Figure 6.5 shows the reliabilities (or yields).

Figures 6.6 and 6.7 show the comparison of reliabilities among the schemes using
STS described until now, the scheme using double tracks (DBT), and the scheme
using a single spare plane, which are denoted as 2p-1t(N), 2p-2t(N), and 1p(N),
respectively for arrays with logical sizes of $N \times N \times N$. 2p-1t(N) and 2p-2t(N) use
the same number of spares $2N^2$ but 2p-2t(N) uses double switches as well as double

Fig. 6.4 Survival rate of
array

Fig. 6.5 Reliability of array

Fig. 6.6 Comparison among
reliabilities of $8 \times 8 \times 8$
arrays

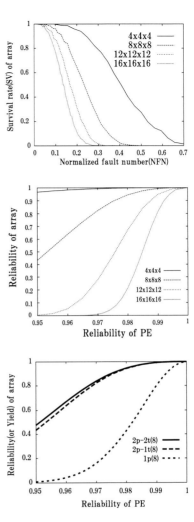

tracks in the direction of X-axis in comparison with 2p-1t(N). From the figures, we
can see that the reliabilities of 2p-1t(N) and 2p-2t(N) are almost the same though the
hardware overhead of 2p-1t(N) is a half of that of 2p-2t(N). The reliability of 1p(N)
which uses a half of spares of 2p-1t but the same numbers of tracks and switches as
those of 2p-1t(N) is much less than that of 2p-1t(N).

Fig. 6.7 Comparison among
reliabilities of $16 \times 16 \times 16$
arrays

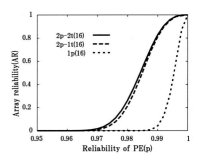

6.2   Spares on Six Faces

Here, using Hopfield-type neural network model, we present an algorithm for reconstructing 3D mesh processor arrays using single-track switches where spare processors are laid on the six surfaces of a 3D array and show its effectiveness in terms of structure rate and computing time by computer simulation.[2] Next, we show how the algorithm can be realized by a digital neural circuit. It consists of subcircuits for finding candidate c-paths, deciding whether the neural system reaches a stable state and at the time the system energy is minimum, and subcircuits for neurons. Since the state transitions are done in parallel, the circuit will be able to find a set of c-paths for faulty PEs very quickly.

6.2.1   Architecture

To augment a 3D mesh into the 3D fault tolerant model, spare PEs are added on the surface of an array as shown in Fig. 6.8, and a single track and a switch with six ports are laid between a PE and each of its six neighbors in the X_-, X_+, Y_-, Y_+, Z_- and Z_+ directions as shown in Fig. 6.9a where each switch takes 13 states as shown in (b).

Fig. 6.8 3D mesh array with
spares on six faces

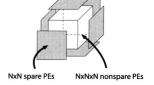

---

[2] The content in this subsection is written, based on the content in the paper [9] (Copyright(C)2022) published from IEICE.

Fig. 6.9   a 3D mesh array
using $1\frac{1}{2}$-track switches and
b States of a switch

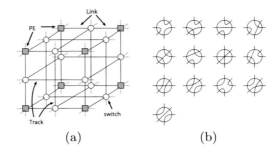

(a)   (b)

A track runs horizontally (vertically) between every two adjacent rows (columns)
of PEs, and switches are laid at the cross-points of links and tracks.

For the restructuring, we assume that faulty PEs are converted into elements
connecting its two ports in either of X, Y or Z directions (see Fig. 6.1), i.e., passed
in either directions.

For an array of size $(N + 2) \times (N + 2) \times (N + 2)$, we assign an index to a PE
as follows. The index $(0, 0, 0)$ is assigned to the PE located at the most north (the
most Y_-), the most west(the most X_-) and the most Z_- direction. The index (i, j, k)
is assigned to the PE located at the i-th counted from the most north to the south, the
j-th from the most west to the east and the k-th from the most Z_- to Z_+ (see Fig.
6.2(b)). PE indexed (i, j, k) is denoted as PE(i, j, k).

The restructuring strategy is as follows.

If PE(i, j, k) is faulty, the following process is executed toward a spare PE on
a surface. The faulty PE(i, j, k) is replaced by an adjacent healthy PE(i', j', k'),
which in turn is replaced by the next adjacent healthy PE(i'', j'', k''), and so on.
This replacement is repeated until a healthy spare PE is used. A sequence of the
PE's indices defined by the above process is c-path which is straight. For each faulty
nonspare PE(i, j, k), there are six possible straight c-paths.

From convenience of description, the north, south, west, east, Z_- and Z_+ directions are denoted as 1, 2, 3, 4, 5, and 6, respectively. The d-directional c-path from a
faulty nonspare PE(i, j, k), is denoted as (i, j, k, d). Further, the intersection relation
and near-miss are defined as in 2D.

Then, decision whether a given faulty pattern is repairable or not by the concept of
c-path is done according to the repairability condition in 2D case defined in Property
3.10 with the inhibition of intersection among c-paths. (Refer to [1]).

6.2.2   Neural Algorithm

We describe a neural algorithm for reconstructing 3D mesh arrays using $1\frac{1}{2}$-track
switches with PE faults in such a way that it may be realized by a digital circuit.

A Hopfield-type neural network is used where six neurons v_{ijkd}'s, $1 \leq d \leq 6$,
are arranged around each nonspare PE(i, j) to decide the directions of c-paths

Fig. 6.10 Distribution of
neurons and the relation
between a c-path and a firing
neuron

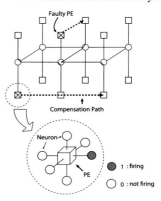

(i, j, k, d)'s ($1 \leq d \leq 6$). Each neuron can be in one of two possible states, either 0 or 1. Then the network will be constructed such that firing of the neuron v_{ijkd}, that is, v_{ijkd}=1 indicates that the c-path (i, j, k, d) exists as shown in Fig. 6.10.

Definition 6.1 The function $CP(i, j, k, d)$=1 ($1 \leq i \leq$ N, $1 \leq j \leq$ N, $1 \leq k \leq$ N, $1 \leq d \leq 6$) if (i, j, k, d) is a candidate c-path for the faulty nonspare PE(i, j, k), and zero otherwise.

Definition 6.2 The function $I(i, j, k, d, x, y, z, e)$=1 if the c-paths (i, j, k, d) and (x, y, z, e) are in intersection relation, and zero otherwise.

Definition 6.3 The function $N_m(i, j, k, d, x, y, z, e)$=1 if the c-paths (i, j, k, d) and (x, y, z, e) are in near-miss relation, and zero otherwise.

The state of the neuron v_{ijkd} at time t is denoted as $v_{ijkd}(t)$. Let $w_{ijkd,xyze}$ be the weight of the link connecting the neurons v_{ijkd} and v_{xyze}, and let θ_{ijkd} be the constant bias of the neuron v_{ijkd}. The state of the network at time t is denoted by the vector $V(t) = \{v_{ijkd}(t)\}$. Then the state of the neuron v_{ijdk} at time $(t + 1)$ is computed by

$$v_{ijkd}(t + 1) = f(u_{ijkd}(t)) \tag{6.1}$$

$$u_{ijkd}(t) = \sum_{x,y,z,e} w_{ijkd,xyze} \cdot v_{xyze}(t) + \theta_{ijkd} \tag{6.2}$$

where $f(x) = 1$ if $x > 0$, and 0 otherwise.

The energy of the neural network at time t is defined as

$$E(V(t)) = -\frac{1}{2} \sum_{i,j,k,d} \sum_{x,y,z,e} w_{ijkd,xyze} \cdot v_{ijkd}(t) \cdot v_{xyze}(t)$$

$$- \sum_{i,j,k,d} v_{ijkd}(t) \cdot \theta_{ijkd} + K_{const} \tag{6.3}$$

To solve the problem to determine a set of c-paths covering all the faulty PEs, which satisfies the repairability condition in Property 3.10 with the inhibition of intersection among c-paths, we formulate three cost functions C_1, C_2 and C_3.

C_1 is defined as taking the minimum value 0 if no c-paths corresponding to neurons whose states are 1's intersect each other, and otherwise a positive value. C_1 is written as follows.

$$C_1 = \frac{A_1}{2} \sum_{i,j,k,d} \sum_{x,y,z,e} (v_{ijkd} \cdot v_{xyze}) \cdot I(i, j, k, d, x, y, z, e) \qquad (6.4)$$

where the parameter A_1 is an appropriate positive constant.

C_2 takes the minimum value 0 when only one c-path is selected among candidates for c-paths for each faulty nonspare PE, and the positive value otherwise. C_2 is written as follows.

$$C_2 = \frac{A_2}{2} \sum_{i,j,k} \left(\sum_d v_{ijkd} \cdot CP(i, j, k, d) - 1 \right)^2 \qquad (6.5)$$

where A_2 is an appropriate positive constant.

C_3 takes the minimum value 0 if no c-paths corresponding to neurons whose states are 1's are in near-miss relation with each other, and otherwise a positive value. C_3 is written as follows.

$$C_3 = \frac{A_3}{2} \sum_{i,j,k,d} \sum_{x,y,z,e} (v_{ijkd} \cdot v_{xyze}) \cdot N_m(i, j, k, d, x, y, z, e) \qquad (6.6)$$

where A_3 is an appropriate positive constant.

Then, the energy function E is defined as

$$E = C_1 + C_2 + C_3 \qquad (6.7)$$

Comparing (6.3) and (6.7), the following network parameters are obtained where $K_{const} = \frac{A_2}{2} \cdot N_F$ and N_F is the number of faulty nonspare PEs.

$$\begin{aligned}
w_{ijkd,xyze} = &-A_1 \cdot (1 - \delta_{ix}\delta_{jy}\delta_{kz}) \cdot I(i, j, k, d, x, y, z, e) \\
&-A_2 \cdot \delta_{ix}\delta_{jy}\delta_{kz}(1 - \delta_{de}) \\
&\cdot CP(i, j, k, d) \cdot CP(x, y, z, e) \\
&-A_3 \cdot N_m(i, j, k, d, x, y, z, e)
\end{aligned} \qquad (6.8)$$

$$\theta_{ijkd} = \begin{cases} \frac{A_2}{2} \cdot CP(i, j, k, d) & \text{if PE } (i, j, k) \text{ is faulty} \\ 0 & \text{otherwise} \end{cases} \qquad (6.9)$$

where $\delta_{ab} = 1$ if $a = b$, 0 otherwise.

The next state of the neural network $V(t + 1)$ is computed from the current state by evaluating Eq. (6.1) at a subset S of neurons. The modes of operation are determined by the method by which the set S is selected in each time interval. If the computation is performed at a single neuron in any time interval, that is, $|S| = 1$ ($|S|$ denotes the number of elements in the set S), then we say that the network is operating in a *serial* mode. If the computation is performed in all neurons at the same time, then we say that the network is operating in a *fully parallel* mode. All the other cases such that $1 < |S|$ are called parallel modes of operation. The set S can be chosen at random or according to some deterministic rule.

A state $V(t)$ is called *stable* if and only if $V(t') = V(t)$ for all $t' > t$. Then the following fact is known. (For the proof refer to [10] or [11]).

Theorem 6.1 *1. Assume that the network is operating in a serial mode and $W = \{w_{ijkd,xyze}\}$ is a symmetric matrix with the elements of the diagonal being nonnegative. Then the network will always converge to a stable state.*
2. Assume that the network is operating in a fully parallel mode and W is a symmetric matrix. Then the network will always converge to a stable state or to a cycle of states of length 2.

From Eq. (6.8) and the definition of $N_m(i, j, k, d, x, y, z, e)$, it is seen that $w_{ijkd,xyze} = 0$ for $ijkd = xyze$, that is, the elements of the diagonal are all zeros, and W is symmetric. Since these satisfies the conditions of the network in Theorem 6.1, the network will always converge to a stable state if it is operating in a serial mode. However, the state change in a serial mode requires $6N^3$ state changes of neurons for a single state change of the network with sizes of $N \times N \times N$ since there are $6N^3$ neurons. This consumes the time proportional to the sizes of the mesh-arrays in hardware realization. But as described in the following, for the neural network defined in Eqs. (6.8) and (6.9) a single state change through the neurons of the network can be performed in constant times of parallel operations while it will always converge to a stable state.

Definition 6.4 A weighted graph is a graph to whose edge numbers called weights are assigned. A weighted graph will be called k-partite if its node set V can be partitioned into k subsets $V_1, V_2, ...,$ and V_k such that there is no edge with nonzero weight connecting any two nodes in V_i ($1 \leq i \leq k$).

A neural network can be considered a weighted graph whose nodes are neurons, and edges are the weighted links connecting neurons.

Theorem 6.2 *Assume that a neural network Net is k-partite as in Definition 6.4. Then the state of Net after a single state change through the neurons computed by such a serial mode that first all the neurons in V_1 are selected one after another, and next similarly those in V_2 and finally those in V_k are selected is the same as that by such a parallel mode that $V_1, V_2, ...,$ and V_k are selected in this order.*

Proof *This is clearly seen from the fact that the output of a neuron in V_i computed by Eq. (6.1) does not influence on the input of any neuron in V_i.*

Property 6.2 If the neural network constructed as in Eqs. (6.8) and (6.9) will be considered a weighted graph whose nodes are the neurons and edges are the weighted links connecting the neurons, it is 6-partite.

Proof From the definitions of the functions I and N_m, $I(i, j, k, d, x, y, z, d) = N_m(i, j, k, d, x, y, z, d) = 0$. Hence, $w_{ijkd,xyzd}=0$ in Eq. (6.8). This implies that there is no edge with nonzero weight connecting any two nodes in $\{v_{ijkd} | 1 \leq i, j, k \leq N\}$.

From Theorem 6.2 and Property 6.2, we have the following property.

Property 6.3 A single state change through the neurons of the neural network constructed as in Eqs. (6.8) and (6.9) can be performed in six times of parallel operations while it always converges to a stable state.

When a stable state has been reached from an initial one, the energy function takes globally (only if the given fault pattern is repairable) or locally minimum value. From the way of the construction of the neural network as in Eqs. (6.8) and (6.9), we can easily have the following property.

Property 6.4 The energy of the neural network takes the minimum 0 if and only if the corresponding stable state implies a set of c-paths in the array which satisfies the repairability condition.

From the consideration above, we have the neural algorithm as follows.

Neural algorithm

1. Decide the functions $CP(i, j, k, d)$, $I(i, j, k, d, x, y, z, e)$ and $N_m(i, j, k, d, x, y, z, e)$.
2. Assign an initial state of the network $V(0) = (0\ 0 \cdots 0)$.
3. Set an appropriate number to $N_{timeout}$ (≥ 1), and let $m = 1$.
4. Make a state transition through all the neurons so that for $d(1 \leq d \leq 6)$ the states of all the neurons corresponding to the c-paths in the d-direction are concurrently computed from the current states by evaluating Eq. (6.1) at the subset $\{v_{ijkd} | 1 \leq i, j, k \leq N\}$.
5. If the network energy at the stable state is the minimum 0, the system is repairable and the c-paths are determined by the neuron's states which are 1's, and go to Step 7. Otherwise, let $m = m + 1$, and go to Step 6.
6. If $m \leq N_{timeout}$, set the network state to an *appropriate one*, and go to Step 3. Otherwise, the fault pattern is regarded as unrepairable and go to Step 7.
7. The end.

In the next section, we will set the bit-wise inverse of the stable state in Step 5 to *appropriate one* in Step 6 from the easiness of hardware implementation.

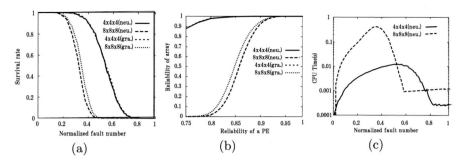

Fig. 6.11 **a** Survival rates, **b** array reliabilities, and **c** computation time by the software algorithm

6.2.3 Simulation Results

We have performed computer simulations for the neural network operating in such a parallel mode that the neurons in the directions 1, 2, 3, 4, 5, and 6 are selected in this order where the neural network is assumed to be fault-free.

Figure 6.11a shows the survival rates $SV(k)$ of arrays with the sizes of $N \times N \times N$ for $N = 4$ and 8 where (neu) and (gra) are by the neural algorithm and a graph (exhaustive) algorithm respectively, and the normalized fault number $NFN = \frac{k}{N_s}$ for the numbers of faults k and spares N_s.

Figure 6.11b shows the reliability $R(p, N_t)$ of an array with $N_t (= N^3 + N_s)$ PEs in terms of the reliability p of a PE.

Figure 6.11c shows the computation time when the neural algorithm is simulated by software using an IBM-PC (CPU = Pentium, Clock = 133MHz) and C language, and $N_{timeout} = 5$.

From the results, it is seen that the efficiency of the restructure by the neural algorithm degrades a little in comparison with that by the exhaustive algorithm while the worst computation time by the former is much less(by about two order for arrays with sizes of $8 \times 8 \times 8$) than that by the latter though it is not shown here. Furthermore, our algorithm has an advantage that it can be implemented by hardware as mentioned in the following section while it seems to be difficult to do so for the exhaustive one.

6.2.4 Digital Neural Circuit

In order to design a digital neural circuit for implementing the foregoing algorithm, we will investigate the behavior of state transition of a neuron. For simplicity of explanation, it is said that the neurons of PE(i, j, k) v_{ijkd} and v_{ijke} $(e \neq d)$ are brothers.

We assume that each PE(i, j, k) outputs a fault status signal f_{ijk} such that $f_{ijk}=0$ if it is faulty, and 1 otherwise. The fault status signal in the direction d from a spare

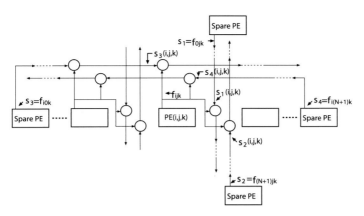

Fig. 6.12 Signal s_d's transmitted along the respective paths, where the round marks are logical AND gates

is denoted as s_d. As shown in Fig. 6.12, the s_d's are transmitted along the respective paths and successively performed logical AND with the fault status signals from PEs on the paths. Let $s_d(i, j, k)$'s denote the signals sent to PE(i, j, k) from the neighbor PEs. Then it is easily seen that the following holds.

Property 6.5 $CP(i, j, k, d) = 1$ if and only if $f_{ijk} = 0$ and $s_d(i, j, k) = 1$.

In what follows, we assume that $A_1 = A_2 = A_3 = 2$ in Eq. (6.8).

From Eq. (6.9), $\theta_{ijkd} = 0$ if PE(i, j, k) is healthy or $CP(i, j, k, d)=0$. From Eq. (6.8), any weight is nonpositive. Hence, we have the following property.

Property 6.6 1. The state of any neuron of a healthy PE after it is computed by the equation (6.1) is always 0.
2. If $CP(i, j, k, d) = 0$, the state of the neuron v_{ijkd} after it is computed by the equation (6.1) is always 0.

From Property 6.6, we will fix the output of the neuron v_{ijkd} to 0 if PE(i, j, k) is healthy or $CP(i, j, k, d) = 0$.

From Eq. (6.8), $w_{ijkd,xyze} \le -2$ if and only if (i, j, k, d) and (x, y, z, e) are in intersection or near-miss, or $(i, j, k) = (x, y, z)$ and $d \ne e$. Further, $\theta_{ijkd}=1$ if PE(i, j, k) is faulty and $CP(i, j, k, d)=1$. Therefore, we have the following property.

Property 6.7 Assume that PE(i, j, k) is faulty and $CP(i, j, k, d)=1$. The state of the neuron v_{ijkd} after it is computed by Eq. (6.1) is 1 if and only if all the followings hold.

1. no brothers of v_{ijkd} are firing, that is, the states of all the brothers are 0's.
2. neither neurons corresponding to c-paths in intersection or near-miss relation with (i, j, k, d) are firing.

Property 6.7 implies that we can use digital operations for computing the states of neurons by Eq. (6.1). Figure 6.13 shows a diode matrix which checks occurrences of c-paths in the intersection relation, basic internal structure of a neuron module and a neuron where the number of diodes in the diode matrix is 24 as shown in Fig. 6.14 where the black dots are connections by diodes whose forward direction is from O_1 to I_2. Though not described here, adjacent horizontal lines or the vertical ones checking occurrences of the near-miss relation are connected by diodes. (b) shows the basic internal structure of a neuron module V_i. If a PE is healthy, the corresponding V_is only work as passing the signals from I_1 to I_2 and O_1 to O_2 since $CP = 0$ from Property 6.5. If a PE is faulty and the c-path in the d-direction can be taken, the neuron in V_d gets the signal from I_1 and outputs to O_2 since $CP = 1$. (c) shows the basic internal structure of a neuron. $J - K$ flip flop stores a present state. A signal for a next state to be stored is given to the J terminal. Hence, the signal indicating stable state is zero if and only if the present state is equal to the next one.

The proposed digital circuit operates in synchronous mode and a single state change of the network through all the neurons is done by six clocks. A clock is given to all the neurons in $\{v_{ijkd}\}$ ($1 \leq d \leq 6$) in the same time. This ensures that the network converges to a stable state by Property 6.3. After each single state change of the network, it must be checked whether the state just before is equal to the present one, and if so, it is decided that the network has reached a stable state. However, as proved in Property 6.8 below, such a check is unnecessary since a neural network reaches a stable state in two transition steps where a transition step corresponds to a single state change of the network through all the neurons.

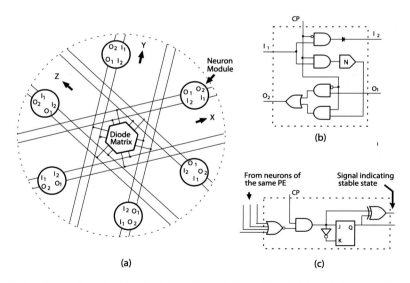

Fig. 6.13 **a** Connection checking the intersection relations, **b** Basic internal structure of V_i, and **c** Basic internal structure of a neuron N

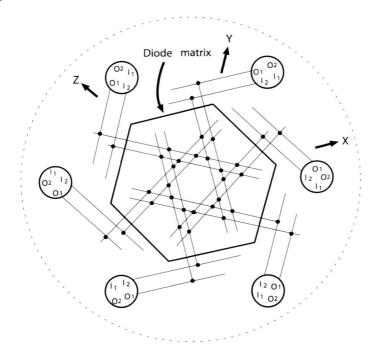

Fig. 6.14 Diode matrix

Property 6.8 Let $V(t) = (v_{1111}(t), \cdots, v_{ijkd}(t), \cdots, v_{NNN6}(t))$ denote the state of the neural network at time t constructed as in Eqs. (6.8) and (6.9) and let $V(t + 1)$ be the state of the network after a single state change through all the neurons computed by Eq. (6.1) from $V(t)$ by a serial mode. Then, the following holds.

1. For any neuron v_{ijkd}, if $v_{ijkd}(t + 1) = 1$, $v_{ijkd}(t') = 1$ for all $t' \geq t + 1$.
2. For any neuron v_{ijkd}, if $v_{ijkd}(t + 1) = v_{ijkd}(t + 2) = 0$, $v_{ijkd}(t') = 0$ for all $t' \geq t + 1$.
3. For all $t' \geq t + 2$, $V(t + 2) = V(t')$, that is, $V(t + 2)$ is a stable state.

Proof

1. From Property 6.7, if $v_{ijkd}(t + 1) = 1$, neither neurons corresponding to c-paths in intersection or near-miss relation with the c-path (i, j, k, d) can fire after $v_{ijkd}(t + 1)$ has become 1. Hence, again from Property 6.7, $v_{ijkd}(t') = 1$ for all $t' \geq t + 1$.
2. From Property 6.6, it is sufficient to consider the case where $PE(i, j, k)$ is faulty and $CP(i, j, k, d) = 1$. Then, $v_{ijkd}(t + 2) = 0$ if and only if at the time when $v_{ijkd}(t + 2)$ is computed, from Property 6.7 there is such a firing neuron $v_{i'j'k'd'}$ that it is a brother of v_{ijkd} or (i', j', k', d') is in a relation of intersection or near-miss with (i, j, k, d). Hence, $v_{i'j'k'd'}(t + 1) = 1$ or $v_{i'j'k'd'}(t + 2) = 1$. Then from

1, $v_{i'j'k'd'}(t') = 1$ for all $t' \geq t+2$. Hence, again from Property 6.7, $v_{ijkd}(t+3) = 0$.

3. This is easily shown from 1 and 2.

From Property 6.8, the check whether the energy of the network is zero is performed after two step transitions through all the neurons. Since a single state change of the neural network through all the neurons is done by six clocks, 12 clocks are sufficient for it to converge to a stable state. Therefore, the neural algorithm will terminate in $12 \times N_{timeout}$ clocks. If $N_{timeout} = 5$ as used in the simulation and the period of the clock is $10\,ns$, the digital neural circuit completes the operation to find a set of c-paths for a fault pattern in $600\,ns$, that is, less than $1\,\mu s$.

From Property 6.7, such a state that there exist firing neurons in intersect or near-miss relations or there exist two or more firing neurons of a nonspare faulty PE is not stable. Therefore, we have the following property.

Property 6.9 The necessary and sufficient condition for that the energy of the network is zero is that at the stable state there is only one firing neuron of each nonspare faulty PE.

Figure 6.15 illustrates a neuron part of the circuit for checking the zero of energy. From Property 6.9, the energy of the network is 0 if and only if the ORed output of all the outputs E's from neurons is 0 at the stable state.

We mentioned that we will set the bit-wise inverse of the stable state in Step 5 to *appropriate one* in Step 6 in the neural algorithm in the previous section.

Figure 6.16 shows the output part of a neuron including the inverse operation of the state. The signal INV inverses the output N_{out}. The signal TRANS causes a state transition of a neuron. It is easily seen that N_{out} after a state transition becomes the same as the signal FIRE.

From the discussion heretofore, in Fig. 6.17 we have the practical circuit for V_i shown in Fig. 6.13a. "Pass-ENin" and "Pass-ENout" correspond to the input and output of the AND gate denoted by the circle in Fig. 6.12, respectively. To "TEeng" is fed the logical ORed signal of "Eng's from all the neurons", to "PE" is a faulty status of a PE, and to from "N_1" to "N_5" are the outputs of brothers of a neuron.

We have confirmed that the proposed system with small sizes works as expected.

Fig. 6.15 Neuron part for checking the zero of energy

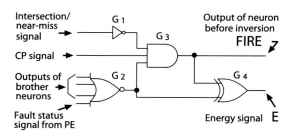

Fig. 6.16 Output part
including inverse operation

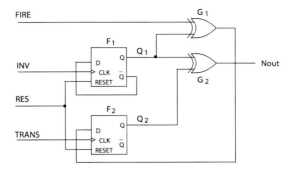

Fig. 6.17 Practical circuit
for a neuron module V_i

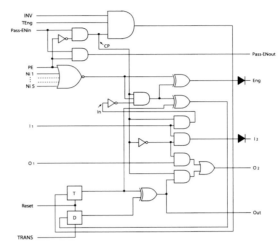

References

1. Chandra, A., Melhem, R.: Reconfiguration in 3D meshes. In: Int'l Workshop on Defect Tolerance in VLSI Systems, pp. 194–202 (1994)
2. Takanami, I., Horita, T.: A built-in self-reconfigurable scheme for 3D mesh arrays. IEICE Trans. Inff Syst. **E82-D**(12), 1554–1562 (1999)
3. Sami, M., Negrini, R., Stefanelli, R.: Fault tolerance techniues for array structures used in supercomputing. IEEE Comput. **19**(2), 78–87 (1986)
4. Kung, S.Y., Jean, S.N., Chang, C.W.: Fault-tolerant array processors using single-track switches. IEEE Trans. Comput. **38**(4), 501–514 (1989)
5. Roychowdhury, V.P., Bruck, J., Kailath, T.: Efficient algorithms for reconstruction in VLSI/WSI Array. IEEE Trans. Comput. **39**(4), 480–489 (1989)
6. Varvarigou, T.A., Roychowdhury, V.P., Kailath, T.: Reconfiguring processor arrays using multiple-track models: the 3 - tracks - 1 - spare - approach. IEEE Trans. Comput. **42**(11), 1281–1293 (1993)
7. Horita, T., Takanami, I.: A built-in self-reconfiguration approach for partitioned mesh-arrays using neural algorithm. IEICE Trans. Inf. Syst. **E79-D**(8), 1160–1167 (1996)
8. Horita, T., Takanami, I.: An efficiently reconfigurable architecture for mesh arrays with PE and link faults. IEICE Trans. Inf. Syst. **E80-D**(9), 879–885 (1997)

9. Takanami, I., Nakamura, S., Horita, T.: Self-Reconstruction of 3D mesh array wiyh $1\frac{1}{2}$-track switches by digital neural circuits. IEICE Trans. Electron. **E82-C**(9), 1678–1686 (1999)
10. Goles-Chacc, E., Fogelman-Soulie, F., Pellegrin, D.: Decreasing energy functions as a tool for studying threshold networks. Discr. Appl. Math. **12**, 261–277 (1985)
11. Bruck, J.: On the convergence properties of the Hopfield model. Proc. IEEE **78**(10), 1579–1585 (1990)
12. Hopfield, J.J.: Neural networks and physical systems with emergent collective computational abilities. Proc. Nat. Acad. Sci. USA **79**, 2554–2558 (1982)
13. Yung, M.W., Little, M.J., Etchells, R.D., Nash, J.G.: Redundancy for yield enhancement in the 3-D computer. Proc. Int'l Conf. WSI 73–82 (1989)
14. Dutt, S., Hayers, J.P.: Some practical issues in the design of fault-tolerant multiprocessors. IEEE Trans. Comput. **41**(5), 588–598 (1992)
15. Mazumder, P., Jih, Y.S.: Restructuring of square processor arrays by builtin self-repair circuit. IEEE Trans. Comput.-Aided Design. **12**(9), 1255–1265 (1993)
16. Takanami, I., Kurata, K., Watanabe, T.: A neural algorithm for reconstructing mesh-connected processor arrays using single-track switches. Proc. Int'l Conf. WSI 101–110 (1995)
17. Carson, J.: The emergence of stacked 3-D silicon and its impact on microelectronics systems integration. Proc. Int. Conf. Innovative Syst. Silicon, 1–8 (1996)
18. Shigei, N., Miyajima, H., Murashima, S.: On efficient spare arrangements and an algorithm with relocating spares for reconfiguring processor arrays. IEICE Trans. Fundament. **E80-A**(6), 988–995 (1997)
19. Kurino, H., Matsumoto, T., Yu, K.-H., Miyakawa, N., Itani, H., Tsukamoto, H., Koyanagi, M.: Three-dimensional integration technology for real time microvision systems. Proc. Int. Conf. Innovat. Syst. Silicon 203–212 (1997)
20. Jain, V.K., Horiguchi, S.: VLSI considerations for TESH: A new hierarchical interconnection network for 3-D integration. IEEE Trans. VLSI Syst. **6**(3), 346–353 (1998)
21. Stephen Lacy, W., Cruz-Rivera, J.L., Scott Wills, D.: The offset cube: A three-dimensional multicomputer network topology using through-wafer optics. IEEE Trans. Parallel Distribut. Syst. **9**(9), 893–908 (1998)
22. Horita, T., Takanami, I.: An efficient method for reconfiguring the 1 trackswitch mesh array. IEICE Trans. Inf. Syst., **E82-D**(12), 1545–1553 (1999)
23. Horita, T., Takanami, I.: Fault tolerant processor arrays based on the 1 track switches with flexible spare distributions. IEEE Trans. Comput. **49**(6), 542–552 (2000)
24. Horita, T., Takanami, I.: An FPGA implementation of a self-reconfigurable system for the 1 track-switch 2-D mesh array with PE faults. IEICE Trans. Inf Syst. **E83-D**(8), 1701–1705 (2000)
25. Jigang, W., Zhu, L., He, P., Jiang, G.: Reconfigurations for processor arrays with faulty switches and links, 15th IEEE/ACM Int, Symp. on Cluster. In: Cloud and Grid Computing, pp. 141–148 (2015)
26. Junyan, Q., Zhide, Z., Tianlong, G., Lingzhong, Z., Liang, C.: Optimal reconfiguration of high-performance VLSI subarrays with network flow. IEEE Trans. Parallel Distribut. Syst. 3575–3587 (2016)
27. Qian, J., Mo, F., Ding, H., Zhou, Z., Gu, Lingzhong Z., Zhongyi, Z.: A improved algorithm for accelerating reconfiguration of VLSI array. Int. VLSI J. **79**, 124–132 (2021)
28. Ding, H., Qian, J., Huang, B., Zhao, L., Zai, Z.: Flexible scheme for reconfiguring 2D mesh-connected VLSI subarrays under row and column rerouting. J. Parallel Distribut. Comput. **151**, 1–12 (2021)

Printed in the United States
by Baker & Taylor Publisher Services